God's Word in Culture

God's Word in Culture

by
Elena Scott Whiteside

American Christian Press
New Knoxville, Ohio 45871
U.S.A.

International Standard Book Number 0-910068-51-8
American Christian Press
The Way International
New Knoxville, Ohio 45871
© 1983 by The Way International
Printed in the United States of America

To my son,
Nicholas Whiteside

TABLE OF CONTENTS

PART TWO—IT IS WRITTEN: ESSAYS IN CULTURE

PREFACE

This collection contains two series of essays on the theme of the Word of God in Culture. The first series was written in 1976 and appeared in *The Way Magazine* in five installments, January/February through September/October 1977, under the title "Word-Centered Culture." Here, the series is edited back to its original three-part structure.

The second series was completed in January 1979 and includes five essays entitled "It Is Written: Essays in Culture." This series grew out of the first in continuing to explore the theme of a life-style, a culture, firmly grounded on the Word of God.

It is the author's desire and prayer that these essays serve to initiate thoughts along the line of God's Word in application and to inspire God's people to greater vision and greater productivity from the wellspring of God's matchless Word at the heart of their lives.

ELENA SCOTT WHITESIDE

ACKNOWLEDGMENTS

Although finally only one person lifts the pen to commit words to paper, many, many people contribute invaluably to any written work. Many have contributed to this book also—some I have met and some, I have not. I am deeply thankful to all those who have prayed, believed and desired to see the Word move over the world along any available avenue. Most particularly, I am thankful to Josephine Joreski who patiently listened to me lay out the whole idea; to Pam Craley who faithfully heard me read each chapter before the ink dried; to Walter Cummins, David Craley, Susan Miller and Beth Lowder who encouraged me in moments when my heart faltered; to Glenda Sue Cole who willingly typed up the whole manuscript and to all the editors, typists, proofreaders and artists who have prepared this manuscript for publication. Without such wonderful people and others not mentioned by name on the team, this book would not be in your hands today. However, I am most thankful to The Teacher, Dr. Victor Paul Wierwille, who taught me God's Word that opened my heart, ignited my life and gave me something to say.

Part One

Word-Centered Culture

Essay One

The Greatest Romantic, The Greatest Adventurer

As a student in college, I once studied the romantic period of the nineteenth century. Some of its giants in poetry were Byron, Shelley, Keats, Wordsworth in England; in painting, Gericault and Delacroix in France; in music, Chopin, Liszt, Tschaikovsky— among many, many others in all areas of art. Their works exhibited certain characteristics which are associated with "romanticism": color, texture, movement, psychological timing, action, adventure, variety, heroism, emotionally piercing sensuality and violence. Sometimes their works reached dramatic and monumental grandeur and at other times their works were intensely, anguishingly personal.

History moves in waves. Men's works of any period reflect the thoughts, ideals and perceptions of the times. Many qualities about romanticism appealed to me, but I saw one underlying theme which far outweighed all its appealing qualities. A strong undercurrent of death pervades and sometimes totally dominates these works. The excitement and outward beauty of spectacle sooner or later reveals the ever-present thrill to kill. And many of the artists themselves died young, in the prime of life, by suicide or in other strange, unnatural circumstances.

After studying the works of many of these people, I formed an opinion and made a solemn judgment. (After all, I was all of eighteen.) I ruled romanticism out of the realm of my acceptable thoughts. I rejected the movement and even endeavored to drop the word "romantic" from my vocabulary, so negatively impressed was I by the underlying death theme of the romantic movement.

As history evolves, in response to a certain movement a countermovement appears. In the nineteenth century, the countermovement to romanticism was realism. Instead of the heroic battles with heroic figures of antiquity, the realist painters, such as Millet, Courbet and Constable chose for their subject matter the common man, common activities, the poor farmer working in his fields, or landscape in its simplicity.

In literature, prose rose to dominance over poetry. The great realist novelists emerged: Zola, Tolstoi, Dickens, among many others. The realist movement bent over backwards to present the common, the plain, the mundane, the everyday, day after day; the realist relished in giving the cold, honest, detailed facts no matter how simple, or sordid, or morbid ad infinitum.

Ah, but there's the rub. Whereas romanticism led to death amongst bursts of flames, drama, excitement and anguish, realism, carried to the extreme, faded to death with a whimper, strangled in the monotony of plain, old, common, daily details. And so, with a sigh,

I laid aside realism also in those days. After that there was not much left.

But wait—today a light glows on the horizon. It is steadily coming towards us. It is increasing, waxing greater and greater, brighter and brighter. Light makes manifest all. Yes, it is the Word of God! Praise the Lord, now we can see something.

Look! The romanticism and realism of the nineteenth century were none other than a very familiar theme in new, glittering garb. Why, they were simply a modern re-emergence of the Epicureans and the Stoics from Athens in the days of Paul! (Consider Acts 17:18.) Stripped of their costumes, there they are: gluttony to death, or abstinence to death.

The same two solutions that were offered in the first century reappeared in the nineteenth century in new disguises, as if to say: "Look at me for answers. I am different. I am entirely new." Yet, we see they are the same two extremes. How wonderful that the light of God's Word allows us to recognize the basic truth behind their flashy exteriors.

But wait. There is even greater truth in the air than the prince of the power of the air. Yes, the greater truth fills the heavens and the earth. For we know from the Word of God that the god of this world is never original. He can only imitate, only counterfeit what the true God has formed, made and created. Therefore, romanticism and realism, these worldly movements, must be the counterfeits of something genuine, something far superior. And they are.

The Adversary is so ugly that he uses truth (in part) and uses light (in part) to draw people to himself, into the snare of his darkness. (Without the light, people would not be drawn.) The truth and light in these works are what appeal to us, interest and excite us. But in the hands of the Adversary, these part-truths are manipulated toward depression, death and destruction. It is he who steals and kills and destroys in any way he can.

What are the wonderful, appealing qualities of romanticism? Why, the high action, the richness of color, the variety of textures, the intense personality, the movement, the very juice of scintillating life. Yes, the excitement, the thrill, the breathless moment-by-moment enjoyment of being alive and an awareness of the moment. Do you recognize these? They are the very qualities of life!

And in realism what are the arresting qualities? There is the stability, the faithfulness, the care of small detail overlooking absolutely nothing, bringing the simple to light, the solidity of foundation, the enjoyment and appreciation of nature, the simple in everything. Do you recognize these? Where have you seen them before? That's it. In the Book, the Book of Life.

We can cast aside the counterfeits. We can turn our eyes to the genuine which so far exceeds in brilliance, variety and imagination. We can build genuine vision from the Book, the whole Book.

For God, the true and living God, our Father and the Father of our Lord Jesus Christ—He is the supreme, original Romantic. And He Himself is the supreme, unsurpassed Realist. Yes, He is Life!

Our Father is the supreme Romantic, the supreme

Adventurer. Knowing all things He alone can afford to be recklessly right. He alone can afford to surprise, to astound, to flabbergast. He is not bound. What greater adventure to embark upon—knowing all things that were to be—than to create the heavens and the earth, to make man, to put up with the vast panorama over centuries of human unbelief and aimlessness, bringing all to the good? What an immense adventure!

Who else could think up a universe? Who else could conceive of blowing the Red Sea apart with the blast of His nostrils? Who could imagine the variety and forms of planets and animals and people? of talking through an ass's mouth? or of overturning mountains by their roots? of trees clapping their hands? of collapsing a city at the blast of a few trumpets?

Who could ever imagine a few printed words guiding people from death unto eternal life (Romans 10:9 and 10)? Who else could imagine raising Jesus Christ from the dead, propelling him through the heavens to His own right hand where, two thousand years later, he still lives and is seated. Who could think up the Body of Christ—one spirit, yet so many members scattered through eras of history, through miles of space, and still one Body with one head?

Who else? Who else? And these are but a few examples of His utterly unfathomable, wildly unbelievable, heady imagination. No wonder we can stand back in awe when we consider that we have been privileged to participate in the thrill of so immense and rich a life—His grand, majestic, heroic, dynamic, ever-changing-for-the-better Adventure of Life.

For He has given us power to participate in this life,

to miss nothing of whatever we are willing to handle. He has plunged us midstream into the most exciting adventure ever conceived. And when one of us lifts a little finger for Him, somewhere in the universe stars collide and fall.

There you are—a taste of something greater than romanticism. The romanticism of the world simply pales before this spectacle.

And He, God, is also the original, the greatest Realist. He has not overlooked a single detail of the Creation; He has thought through every life cycle of every creature and woven them all together. He is more real than what our five senses perceive around us. Being perfect, He is always faithful, solid, always to be counted on. He is ever-present, everywhere. He misses absolutely nothing. He is our solid Rock, impossible to chip or even to scratch—stable, constant, unmoving, continuous.

What or who can be more real than He? Facing all the future with His ever-present equanimity, never budging from His purpose which is, quite simply, the pleasure of His own good will. What a foundation! What a Rock! What a Realist!

And so, my friends, the doors of my mind were recently flung open by the light. Light poured in and fresh air brought my thoughts to bloom.

Welcome back to my life, Romanticism (the genuine)! Welcome back, Realism (the genuine)! Welcome back, Adventure unlimited, unparalleled— for "eye hath not seen, nor ear heard, neither have entered into the heart of man, the things which God hath prepared for them that love him. But God hath revealed *them* unto us by his Spirit: for the Spirit searcheth all things, yea, the deep things of God'' (I Corinthians 2:9 and 10).

Oh God, our Father, what can these deep things be? We are waiting, watching breathlessly. And while we wait, let us immerse our minds in the oceans of His thoughts so that we also may dream His dreams, perceive His visions, that we may constantly prove His power. We desire no other.

Truly, His heart is an open book. And we today, through this ministry, have had the Book revealed to the eyes of our understanding. His visions are in there—look at them. His dreams are in there—seek them out. His thoughts are laid out word upon word, line upon line, statute upon statute. Ah, do not miss a stroke, a jot or a tittle, for even the smallest particle of His Word abounds in life. Do not miss the Greatest Adventure ever told—or for that matter, untold.

For He exhorts us to be imitators of Him. Then we too can be renewed-mind romantics. We too can be unmoveable, solid realists. We too can be the unflung adventurers of this age. He will take us with Him as far as we care to go.

Essay Two

The Word in Culture

When I first sat through the Power for Abundant Living class several years ago in Rye, New York, I had been working for two years as a free-lance writer. Writing poetry had pleased me the most, but I soon learned that no one wanted to pay me for poetry. So I expanded into research and writing in an area where I had considerable background. I wrote because I enjoyed it.

Right after taking the Foundational Class, I became totally engrossed in God's Word and for several months immersed myself in reading only the Bible and ministry materials. As the months went by, however, and my deepest thirst for spiritual knowledge began to be quenched for the first time in my life, my mind again wandered more and more often to the blank page and the pen.

At this point, a conflict emerged in my mind. On the one hand, I was convinced that the Word of God was God's Word and that He was the greatest author ever. Furthermore, I was sure that in the Bible (through His holy men in history) He had already said everything that needed to be said. My conclusion: "Why write anything? What could I write? It has all been said. If I

write, I am presuming that more needs to be said."
And that struck me as presumptuous—to desire to add
to God.

This argument made sense to me, and I concluded
that any writing on my part—except perhaps in-depth
research, about which I did not yet know enough to
begin—would be vain, egotistical, seeking to bring
glory to myself.

This line of thought would have been final, except
that days are long and I often came back to the fact that
I really enjoyed writing. Besides that, I also enjoyed
reading poetry, novels and essays (other than the
Word) that also increased my knowledge, built my vision, opened my insight and inspired me to develop my
abilities and talents.

And I was not alone with my conflict. For I met
others now and then with serious thoughts of being
painters, musicians, dancers or businessmen on the
one hand, yet feeling on the other hand that God's will
for them was to "keep in the Word," which in my
thoughts meant: spending day after day in some
unassuming garret, wearing the same unassuming attire, working, reading and studying the Bible fifteen
hours a day, interrupted only to run to a fellowship two
or three hours every night.

Do not ask me now where I got this gray image of the
more abundant life. Looking back I do not recall
anyone teaching this. (The mind works in peculiar
ways sometimes.) But at that time I could not reconcile
what looked like a vain, egotistic, worldly desire to
write on the one hand, with what seemed to me to be
God's will on the other hand.

It is at this point that I decided to look for answers in His Word. (Now, that is always right.) Was there a place for writing? And for that matter, for the other arts? For culture? If so, how did art and culture fit with the Word? Could I go in the direction of writing and still be within God's will?

As I began to work these areas in the Word on and off over the months and years, the truth that dawned little by little (God so gently opens our eyes, lest we fall backwards over the immensity of His more abundant life) so set me free, so built my vision and increased my understanding of God, that I would like to share some of these findings here.

To begin with, I shall be defining culture and the arts. Secondly, I will share with you a framework that has helped me to evaluate and understand areas of culture today. In this discussion, I plan to explode a couple of myths that held me in their grip for years. Lastly, I would like to build vision before our eyes of Word-centered culture, from both the Word of God and its potential application today.

CULTURE AND THE ARTS: A DEFINITION

Culture includes all things that man does and makes that are evidenced in the senses realm to either one or several of the five senses. There are the things around us that God made—trees, mountains, the sky, stars, animals, plants and man. We cannot even hope to "make" a tree or even a simple leaf. These are all things that God formed, made and created in the beginning.

But God formed, made and created man with a

mind, an imagination, with various abilities and certain needs. As man stewards his abilities and his surroundings, he brings into evidence things and services that he needs and also enjoys. All these "things" (or goods) and "services" comprise culture.

Starting from the skin out, what we wear is culture. What we eat is culture; how we verbally express ourselves is culture; how we live is culture; how we go to work, whether on a bicycle or in a Rolls Royce, is culture. Whether or not we work is culture; how we spend our leisure time is culture. Whether it's developing a hobby, going to a football game or going to the opera, these all fall under the category of culture—for man has somehow invested himself with his surroundings to produce effects in the senses realm.

All culture at some point begins in man's mind; in most cases he brings these ideas into evidence with his hands. For our thoughts are the seeds of our words and our deeds. These things man does are evidenced to at least one of the five senses, if not several. Cooking, for example, can be seen, touched, tasted, smelled, even sometimes heard (as popcorn popping, or bacon sizzling in the skillet). Music, as another example, is basically heard, although it may also be felt, and, if written down, it can be seen.

Now then, certain areas of culture we *all* share: we *all* eat something, we all wear something, we all live someplace and we all do something. We are not *of* the world, but we do live *in* it. And to live in it, we must all participate in the above activities to a degree.

Other areas of culture are of a more specialized nature. Not everyone likes to write, or read, for that matter. Not everyone likes to paint or have a painting on his wall—he may prefer photographs, or hanging plants, or artifacts, or rope sculpture, or beads, or wallpaper or monochromatic paint.

When I speak of an "area of culture," I am singling out one of man's numerous activities. This will become significant later on in this essay. For example, cooking is an area of culture, as is music, manners, fashion, architecture, interior decorating, industrial design, city planning, writing, sculpture, business, agriculture, government. The list is very long, but it is finite, for man's activities are limited and can be counted. You add whatever you think of. Remember, culture includes all of man's activities which are evidenced in the senses realm.

At this point, I would like to burst one myth that I grew up with, and that is that "culture" is a term of value, a moral judgment. As far back as I can remember, I would hear people say: "So-and-so is very 'cultured'—he travels, goes to the theater, drives a fine car," etc.; or "So-and-so is so 'uncultured' because he is an aborigine, running around the jungles wearing nothing but a string of tiger's teeth around his neck."

Culture is not a value term so that one can be "more" or "less" cultured. Culture is a fact and cultures differ. Culture differs from country to country, from geographic area to geographic area and, within a society, from economic group to economic group or from social group to social group. Culture differs. All culture is acquired. People learn preferences from their surroundings—things and people. Culture is not more or less superior or inferior, even though we may hold strong opinions as to our own personal preferences in life-style.

As you see, what are traditionally referred to as "the arts," or "creative arts" or "fine arts" (usually including painting, sculpture, literature, music, architecture and perhaps others such as theater and dance) are simply various areas of culture. That these arts are somehow better or superior to other human activities—as I was led to believe most of my life—seems to be entirely erroneous.

For the best human activities and artifacts are always those which are *needed* at that time. If one is hungry, the finest masterpiece would not satisfy physical hunger. If there is no house, it's time for the architect, the builder. If the house has been built, perhaps an interior decorator is needed. If a person is already fed, perhaps the need is music or theater. That the arts were always lumped together as somehow superior—all else referred to slightly condescendingly as "handicrafts," "skills," "hobbies" or "interests"—always used to annoy me, but I did not know why.

I Corinthians 12:31 tells us of "the more excellent way" in spiritual matters. That is to walk in the love of God, operating manifestations and gift ministries as they are needed. In culture, pertaining to man's soul life the principle is the same. What is best is what is needed at the time.

Culture is the result of man's soul life, and since God gave each of us a soul as well as a spirit and a body, He must have given it for a purpose. We do not have to look far. According to III John 2, "Beloved, I wish above all things that thou mayest prosper and be in health, even as thy soul prospereth.'' God wants the soul lives of His people to prosper—that His people may be surrounded by an edifying environment and engaged in edifying activities which meet their own as well as others' needs.

So much for defining culture and the arts. We see that all culture is the result of the workings of man's soul life and that culture includes all things man does and makes that are in evidence to at least one of the five senses. And the arts are various areas of culture.

THREE VIEWPOINTS

Anything in the senses realm affects our senses and therefore our minds, our very states of being. It has helped me immensely to distinguish three points of view in considering any work of men's hands. I would like to share this framework with you.

The first point of view from which to look at anything man has done, I have called "spiritual." Anything in evidence in the senses realm either builds our believing or tears it down. To see where something is "spiritually," I ask myself certain questions that help me see: Whom does this glorify? The true God, or the man that made it? Does this build my believing in God's power? Does it turn my mind to some aspect of the more abundant life? Does it increase my understanding or thoughts of God? Or, does it depress, discourage and annoy me? From this point of view, the works of men's hands are basically either light or dark. They either build believing or tear it down.

The second point of view from which to consider any work of men's hands, I have called "technical"—it involves skill. Any work that is accomplished is done with more or less skill. The first time you perform a song, or paint a picture, or write a poem, or type on a typewriter, your results will not be as technically sound, not as skillful, as after you have practiced with your materials ten, twenty, a hundred or a thousand times.

From this technical point of view, the scale of progress goes from less skill to more skill, to a high degree of skill, and then on to various degrees of mastery or artistry. The only way to reach mastery in the technical area is by applying those sound principles of God's Word: *believing* (disciplined action, disciplined practice), *faithfulness* (one must practice week after week, year after year; once is not enough) and finally, *attention to detail* (improvement through practice reveals more and more details which can be constantly improved). The difference between a work of art and a masterpiece is in the attention to detail.

When an individual has reached a high degree of mastery in an area of culture, he then is an artist. And here I would like to explode another myth that held me in bondage for many years. The truth of the matter is that anyone can become an artist in any area of culture. The governing element is a deep and dedicated desire to practice faithfully over a period of time, paying constant attention to improving on minute details in that area. Anyone willing to do this can become an artist.

Throughout my formal schooling I was taught that there were two kinds of people: the artists and the masses. (I went to a liberal arts college, of course.) I learned that the artists had "it" and that no one else did. What they had was unclear to me, and when I inquired of my professors what "it" was, they could not tell me. I was left with the impression that "it" was something one was born with or somehow mysteriously acquired; that "it" was impossible to describe; that "it" was exclusive, mystical, undefinable. But that without "it," anyone was a fool to try.

At that time I had thoughts of becoming a writer and this attitude was particularly discouraging to me. For I thought, if I don't have "it," why even bother to try? And what "it" was, no one could answer, thus building an atmosphere of anxiety (Do I have it? Don't I have it?), of fear (Am I one of the chosen? What if I'm not? How do I know?), and worst of all, great discouragement. For this mystical and exclusive character of the artist took away all my desire even to try, lest I should be fighting destiny.

Not all people are encased in such ignorance, but, believe me, a great door was opened in my mind when I understood that anyone can become an artist in any area of culture. Why? Because this technical point of view is governed by principles, and principles can be taught and they can be learned (as we shall see later in Exodus 35).

The one governing factor in becoming an artist is the individual's deep and dedicated *desire* to learn these principles, practice them faithfully, constantly improving on minute detail until the media or materials have been mastered. In Galatians 5:6 it is written that believing works (is energized) by love. That deep and dedicated desire gives us energy to practice faithfully and to keep on improving.

There is no question that people are born with certain natural abilities, inclinations and talents, such as a sharp ear for music or a quick mind for figures or a good build for dance or athletics. Yet, having these natural abilities does not matter unless they are utilized and developed. How many people do you know with abilities who do not use them? Certainly, it is nice to have them, but having them is not the deciding factor—utilization and development are.

As a matter of fact, very often a particular disability in a person's makeup will act as a catalyst that causes him to organize his energies to overcome it. One example that comes to my mind is the ballerina Moira Shearer. At ten years old she was pigeon-toed and knock-kneed, and everyone told her she did not have the build or body to be a ballerina. She was determined, however, and in Australia where she grew up, she walked to her ballet lessons faithfully. In later life, she became a prima ballerina in the Royal Ballet in London.

You perhaps know of other examples where a seeming handicap or lack of a natural ability simply gave that individual the goal and impetus to overcome, building great skill in the process. It is not what we have, but rather what we do with what we have that determines success. And the governing factor in use is the individual's deep and dedicated desire to invest time and energy in developing that area. Certainly natural abilities exist and are helpful; nevertheless, whether great or not so impressive, they need to be developed.

When I speak of mastery, I mean the display of skill or technique somewhere beyond the point where the dream, vision, image or plan in the mind can be so thoroughly and well thought through that the project completed is exactly as dreamed and intended. This can only be done with a thorough knowledge of media and materials and their exact interaction and effects.

With mastery the individual becomes an artist. A person can be an artist at cooking, at painting, at business, at writing, at hairstyling, at fashion design, at dance, at farming, at nursing, at handling people—you name it. In any field of culture, mastery or artistry is available to those who are willing to apply the sound principles from God's Word. For us, the born-again believers, we all have the same spiritual ability of Christ in us. We have within us the ability to believe to the uttermost. Being an artist in any area is for those who dare to believe.

While we are discussing the "technical" point of view, let me say a word about principles. Principles govern every area of human endeavor. Principles are true—for God set up laws that are natural, physical, chemical, biological, physiological, etc. Although these operate in the natural realm, they are still true.

For example, where in the Word does it say that H_2O makes water? From my reading of the Word, that is not written. Nevertheless, that is true. This is a chemical law. H_2O will make water every time for everybody— whether a child of God, a child of the devil or your basic natural man.

Cooking works by physical and chemical laws primarily. So likewise, for the child of God, the child of the devil or the basic natural man, too much salt will make the soup too salty. That is a chemical law. That is principle. Even though I cannot quote you chapter and verse, these principles can be traced and found in God's order and God's creation.

Let us look at principles in painting as another example. In painting we are dealing with certain basic elements: a two-dimensional surface, line, color, form, texture, composition, perspective, modeling, rhythm, repetition of visual patterns—these all operate by principle. The aim of painting is to make a three-dimensional world on a two-dimensional surface, to make this world within the frame believable so that the viewer—if he gives that world his attention—can enter mentally, thereby allowing himself to be influenced by that world.

These basic elements in painting can be combined with varying degrees of skill. These elements can be used with great mastery so that the world represented is almost irresistible, and consequently, its influence on the viewer, profound. These elements in painting operate by principle. Principle also governs the technical approach to *all* other areas of human endeavor—architecture, music, writing, knitting, business, teaching, carpentry, athletics—every area.

I have taken considerable time to distinguish between the "spiritual" and the "technical" points of view because it is important to realize that a totally dark work can still have a high degree of mastery in technique. And in this technical area one can always learn by study and observation the HOW—how the principles were combined and used to achieve such astounding effects. Principles can be used to disseminate light as well as darkness.

Now then, the reverse is also true. Someone may be born again, may love God's people, desire to bless them; and that is wonderful. Such a person may compose a song or paint a picture, build a building or start a business or become a doctor. However, just because he loves God, he will not necessarily have great proficiency in handling his material unless he also puts forth the time and effort to build skill in that area.

In Luke 16:8, the Lord is speaking a parable: "And the lord commended the unjust steward, because he had done wisely: for the children of this world are in their generation wiser than the children of light." The unjust steward was *wiser* because he had learned and was operating principles in business and human relations. This does not mean that the children of light need to stay ignorant, however. The same principles can be operated by us—the children of light—but they must be learned and practiced.

There is always potential for improvement. Technical skill, artistry, mastery—these are not achieved in a day or perhaps not even in a year. Time and application are required for the born-again believer as well as for the natural man. Nevertheless, with God's ability living within and a knowledge of God's Word, an individual's growth in skill can be astoundingly fast. Remember Isaiah 48:17: "Thus saith the Lord, thy Redeemer, the Holy One of Israel; I *am* the Lord thy God which teacheth thee to profit, which leadeth thee by the way *that* thou shouldest go."

God is faithful to teach us to profit through areas of life where we have understanding. And it is from the "spiritual" and "technical" points of view that we can learn tremendously. BUT only if the Word of God is living in our minds. If it is not, we could be confused by the basic darkness of the world, and our believing could be momentarily weakened until we again allowed the light of the living Word to penetrate our minds.

It is God's Word that makes us able to separate truth from error, and His Word must be living and vibrant in our minds daily in order to receive the profit. Therefore, let me emphasize here the tremendous importance of being grounded and established in the Word and also of continuing in that Word daily, habitually. Often, in looking at a work of men's hands the error is spiritual, but the truth lies in the correct use of principles, in technique.

Now then, enough about "spiritual" and "technical." The third point of view from which to regard anything man does or makes is "opinion." Opinion in itself does not matter. For example, you would like a song while I dislike it. Or, I could like a painting and you dislike it. Opinions differ in taste and preference and do not much matter.

The reason I bring opinion in here, however, is that too often opinion is an excuse for sloppy, lazy thinking. For example, I could say I like this poem and therefore not even bother to notice a very poor handling of words in a certain line. Just because I like it, I might not bother to learn what I can in the "technical" area. Or, in the reverse, perhaps I do not like a certain building design. Too often, an opinion of dislike will cloud the further quest to see what was done expertly in the matter of handling and combining materials and ideas. To avoid being robbed of a potential lesson in learning, then, I have included this category of opinion also.

I hope that by now the distinctions among the spiritual, technical and opinion points of view are clear to you. I would now like to show you an example of this framework in application. I have chosen to apply the framework to a painting. But remember, these distinctions hold for considering anything man does or makes: a piece of music, a book, a poem, a building, a work of sculpture, a dress, a hairdo, an interior, or any service, any part of culture. A painting is advantageous because it can be reprinted here on the page where we can look at it together.

THE THREE VIEWPOINTS ILLUSTRATED IN A PAINTING

This work by the French painter Degas (late nineteenth century) is a "classic." Ballet was a major theme in his works during a later period of his working life. This one is called "The Rehearsal" and hangs in the Frick Collection in New York City. It was a favorite of mine for years before I began to study art and culture in light of God's Word.

Innocent enough, isn't it? The musician in the foreground is playing the violin while three ballerinas (and the leg of a fourth) are practicing études in a light and uncluttered dance studio. Doesn't that look pleasant, uncomplicated in theme and handling?

Now, let us look more carefully. In considering paintings (as well as some writing, sculpture, interiors and architecture, areas of culture where the visual plays a major role), I have found that a most revealing question is: where is the light coming from and what does it illuminate? For without light, there would be NO painting, only a black canvas. Darkness is the absence of light and is unappealing, which is why the Adversary uses truth (in part) and light (in part) to attract interest and hold attention.

All right, where is the light coming from? What does it illuminate here? We are now looking for the spiritual message of this painting. Does it build believing or tear it down? Whom or what does it glorify?

We see immediately that the light enters the picture from the outside and that the entire scene is backlit. The violinist on the foreground plane is the main character. He is the one with whom the viewer identifies and the one who brings the viewer into this world, for he is on the brink of our space and an outsider even to the dancers in the painting. Being backlit, his eyes are darkened. (Yet, I know from the Word that God wants the eyes of our understanding to be enlightened!) These darkened eyes give our main figure a depressed, discouraged, resigned quality. This mood is further emphasized by the limp, almost dead hand, in our direct foreground, by the figure's black, undefined garb, and the whole stance of his body. Why, he is completely limp, all hunched over in his seat (which we do not see); therefore, in the viewer's eyes, nothing is supporting him. In this precarious world, nothing holds up our main figure.

Remember, what you look at long enough, you become. Do you see the effect this figure has on the viewer, even if he is not conscious of it? A dark, dejected, forlorn human form with no support dominates and brings us into this scene.

Now, what about the other figures? They look light and airy enough. They also are backlit. What about their faces? Are these portraits? No, for they are too generalized and yet at the same time rather strange-looking (especially the central face). So we see they are not studies of the beauty and depth of the human face.

What about their bodies? Are they studies in the human form, the glory and beauty of the human body that God made so fearfully and wonderfully? Are they studies in body dynamics or movement? No, the bodies are all covered up. Then why are these figures in the picture? And that dismembered leg in the right foreground. It is very disturbing—it has no body! What are these figures doing in the picture and why in this particular pose?

Note the composition of this picture. The composition is defined by the lines. The entire picture is organized in strong diagonals (floor lines, extended legs) and strong verticals (windows, ballerinas' bodies, bow of the violin). The three ballerinas and the unattached leg merely emphasize and reemphasize the verticals and diagonals. Why?

The giveaway is the orange tights on the ballerina nearest the dominant figure of the violinist. The orange is on the foreground plane (of course, this is not clear on this black and white print, but it is immediately noticeable on the original). The orange legs—emphasizing the vertical and diagonal structure of the picture—actually confine, entrap and hold the main figure in their grip. He is in bondage. He cannot escape. The whole picture is of bondage—the verticals and diagonals confining the dominant, limp, dark, backlit, unenlightened figure in their prison. And the figure in the foreground is the one with whom the viewer identifies.

Well, what is this painting saying spiritually? What is the message? Who is it glorifying? Does it build the viewer's believing or tear it down? Is it presenting some aspect of the more abundant life? Is it showing us something of what the true God makes available to His people? Answer for yourself.

Let me add that I looked at this picture for years, even analyzed it in my studies of art history. It was a favorite. And until I began to study culture and art from the Word of God, I did not see any of the above. In fact, once I knew what I was looking for, I still did not see these things immediately. I had to look, to study, to speak in tongues and ask God to enlighten my understanding before I saw the spiritual message this picture subtly but definitely proclaims.

Now, let us consider the painting from the "technical" point of view. If I were a painter seeking to improve my own handling of materials, I would undoubtedly see much more. However, let me share with you several technical points that I do see here.

First of all, the originality of approach in composition is worth noting. The diagonal-vertical structure is very well handled, well balanced, drawing the viewer into the depth of the world represented. Because it is an untraditional handling, it demands attention. If I were a painter, painting for the true God, I might note that type of structure in my memory as a possible way to handle another theme in an arresting manner demanding attention.

Secondly, the painter has an excellent understanding

of space. The planes and perspective are very clearly defined. The foreground plane—the musician, the orange tights and the leg on the right; the second plane—two ballerinas; the third plane—the middle ballerina; the fourth plane—the windows and the back wall. These distinctly defined planes give this world depth and order, both of which are very satisfying to the eye and generally pleasing. The order is well carried out and one of the most attractive things in the picture. In fact, order is always appealing because all order is of God. Again, if I were a painter I would be reminded of that in organizing my materials on canvas.

Furthermore, the painting is coherent because of repetition on all planes of the basic pattern (vertical-diagonal). Repetition in subtle ways gives coherence and order, both qualities I would want to achieve as a painter. I might also note the use of color, of light, the portraiture, the handling of the human body, the handling of movement, modeling, proportions. For the painter with a trained eye, there might be a few other things to learn technically from this picture that could be useful. The learning might take five minutes or an hour or a day. I cannot tell with this particular picture.

A painter might look for any successful techniques that could help him handle his materials with a higher degree of skill. He would be looking at the HOW, knowing that some of Degas' techniques might be useful in presenting an aspect of the more abundant life, in presenting some image worthy of glorifying the true God. He could bless God's people by setting down images of order, peace, abundance and inspiration according to God's Word.

Now to our third point of view—"opinion." I might like this picture; you might not. So what? If I happen to like it enough to hang it on my wall, that is my business. If you don't like it, thank God it is on my wall, not your wall. Opinion does not matter. You and I could differ, but from the spiritual point of view and from the technical point of view, we are dealing with facts and therefore would have to agree. Spiritually and technically (no matter what our separate opinions), you and I could both learn something from studying this picture. You might observe details I had missed and I might draw valid conclusions you had missed. That is why I have brought in opinion—to make sure, whether you and I like or dislike something man has made or done in the senses realm, we avoid being robbed of the chance to sharpen our spiritual awareness and perception, as well as our thoroughness in observing detail.

I have taken some time to look at this painting with you because I want you to understand what I mean. I used a painting as an example here because it was expedient for the printed page. However, I am dealing with principles, and principles apply in any area of human endeavor.

Although when this framework came to me I began to look for its application in painting, my real interest was to see its application in writing. Therefore, in writing I have gone on to explore the workings of these principles in greater detail. But I know, because they are principles, that they must apply as well in music, architecture, sculpture, city planning, fashion, business—every area of human endeavor.

I would like to close this section of analysis with a

word of caution— caution resulting from my own experience. I am not advocating here that you now throw yourself into all the worldly works of history in your field to analyze them within this framework. The world is spiritually dark and what fellowship hath light with darkness? One needs to proceed with caution. And although darkness cannot quench the light, darkness does absorb some light on the periphery.

This I myself found when I began to study how these principles worked among my old literary heroes— Shakespeare, Dostoevsky, Tagore, St. Exupery, Whitman, Emerson. I began rereading some things to see where they sat spiritually.

Once I had answered that, again through special attention to imagery (light and dark), I began to look consciously for the techniques of writing that were used successfully.

I found that even though I knew what I was looking for, at times I would get involved, slightly depressed, generally discouraged, and sometimes even nauseous. I learned to drop them quickly when I saw the first signs and to immerse my heart and soul in God's Word to be refreshed, to be enlightened, comforted, encouraged. I found it expedient to deal with worldly works only a little at a time, to allow God to teach me. I am thankful to God constantly that I know the source to which to return for revitalization of life and understanding and peace—His Word.

Yes, we have the greatest, most reliable and thorough source from which to learn. We have the Word of God. At the same time, the above framework enabled me to realize greater learning from my surroundings. When I come in contact with worldly works, I am not afraid to confront them. This is why this framework has been useful to me. It has helped me understand more of what is around me and more quickly.

But we are privileged to have the most reliable source from which to learn. If indeed all things pertaining to life and godliness are in the Word as stated in II Peter 1:3, then we can look to learn both basics and particulars in our fields from that Word.

For the writer, of course, the application might seem more obvious. God's Word is the finest example of all forms of writing—short story, novel, journalism, biography, essay, poetry, parable, science fiction, screenplay, drama, etc. It also contains the finest examples of all elements of style: handling of character, setting, plot, imagery, action, word usage, figures of speech, to name a few.

But what about other areas of culture? In the area of music there is a great deal about instruments, occasions, necessity, importance, effects, use, songs. In painting—color is handled in the Word, not to mention the great example of the God-made nature that surrounds us, filled with examples of color and visual images for our study. Architecture—there is considerable material for study in the building of the tabernacle, the Temple, Noah's ark, the new Jerusalem of how people handled their enterprises and the results of that handling. In food or cooking, there is considerable material. In manners, in speech, in clothing (fashion)—why, the list is endless just off the top of my head. The Word must have something to say that can be applied in every area of culture.

Before you ask me about ballet or mechanics, let me handle that. I grant you that *Young's Analytical Concordance* does not list these two, along with many other modern professions and specialties. Deeper study might be required. The Word does not contain a conclusive section on ballet or mechanics.

But what really is involved in ballet? Ballet is the study of time and space, using the human body as a measure. The development of the human body is involved. There is a great deal on the body in the Word. Ballet also involves rhythm, patterns, order, form, music, repetition—all these areas might be worthy of attention.

And mechanics—does it not have to do with the relations between man and materials? Does it not have to do with stewardship of surroundings? Does it not have to do with certain principles in the areas of order, sequence, giving and receiving?

These are some off-the-cuff suggestions from an amateur. Neither ballet nor mechanics is my specialty. But I reiterate my challenge of II Peter 1:3. If God says that "all things that *pertain* unto life and godliness" are in His Word, then surely there must be something that has to do with your area in there. Ask God to help you find it.

Yes, go to the Word in your area of special interest. Study it out. I guarantee it will take you more time than one day. In fact, it may be a lifelong study. God's Word is a way of life. God's Word always reveals more to us the deeper we search it out, as we are ready to receive it.

I cannot overstate the importance of being, staying and growing in that Word—daily. God backs me up on this exhortation. And I have also observed this importance in my own experience. People in professions that require great mental discipline over a period of time need to discipline their lives even more to the Word, to cleave to it constantly. For such areas of endeavor tend to so fill our minds and our time that the Word fades away in our minds almost without our noticing it. BUT THE WORD IS LIFE, and when we allow ourselves to be tricked, even temporarily, we are cutting ourselves off from LIFE itself.

Therefore, let us keep the Word as our primary source of general study as well as study in our particular areas of interest. Let us remind ourselves and each other constantly to continue speaking in tongues and thinking God's thoughts daily. And this we can do by our example: the words of our mouths and the works of our hands—culture.

I hope that the specifics of this section have inspired you to apply these keys to your area of interest. Search the Scriptures for depth of understanding in your field.

THE FIRST-CENTURY CHURCH AND THE TWENTIETH CENTURY

I began this essay by defining culture as anything man does or makes which at some point begins in his mind and which he then brings into evidence in the senses realm. Man cannot bring into being something he does not have within. Man cannot give what he does not have. If the accuracy of the Word is not in a person's heart, he cannot bring it into evidence. He might do some counterfeiting, some imitation, some things that look or sound good, but the accuracy of the Word will NOT be living in the works of his hands.

Let me ask you a question. When in history has the accuracy of God's Word lived among a group of people? Think about that. (We shall be discussing two of these eras later on in this essay.) But perhaps your mind flashed to the first century. All right, what remnants of the culture of the first-century Church do we have today? The greatest, of course, is the Word of God—the Gospels, the Epistles, the entire New Testament. This priceless literature has come down to us today. Praise the Lord! But what else—what architecture, frescoes, tools, other writings, jewelry?

From my studies in history, literature and art history, there is very little Christian art or artifacts from that time. Artifacts began to accumulate in the fifth century (primarily architecture), becoming more numerous in the twelfth and thirteenth centuries and expanding greatly in the Renaissance of the fourteenth and fifteenth centuries. People really got busy, but by then, where were they spiritually? Was the Word of God living in a group of people?

Knowing Satan to be the god of this world, I am not surprised that he poured forth tremendous efforts in perverting man, and thereby *all* of man's works, away from the true Word, away from the Mystery.

We know from Paul's epistles that even before the end of his lifetime the Mystery (Christ in you, the hope of glory; the one Body) was fading into obscurity among the believers. If the Mystery was fading out, forgotten, how could the truth of it be represented in the things men made and did?

Dr. Wierwille has stated that the major reason for the fall of the first-century Church was that they NEVER GOT THE WORD INTO THEIR CULTURE!

What a tremendous thought: a man can never give what he does not have. To get the living Word into one's works, it first would necessarily have to be rooted and grounded in his heart, and then be so bubbling over, so effervescing, that it reaches out into forms over a period of time—enough time for a person to develop a high degree of skill in his field, be it music, painting, writing, architecture, sculpture, etc.

Remember, what we look at, what is around us, either builds our believing (edifies us) or tears down our believing in both subtle and obvious ways. The Word can never come out of a person until it lives within him, lives within him to such a degree that nothing, NOTHING, ABSOLUTELY NOTHING ELSE REALLY MATTERS.

When people enter The Way Corps, they are often asked to put away their musical instruments and to learn and live the Word for the first months or until they realize that nothing else really matters. Our activities are engrossing, fun, interesting, but as long as our pens, paintbrushes, guitars, pianos and cameras have a hold over us, we shall never really be committed to the Word. And as long as we are not totally committed to the Word (*doulos*—bond-slave), the Word will never live in our works.

If the Word does not live in our surroundings—the clothes we wear, the books we read, the furnishings of our homes, the pictures on our walls, the music we play—then little by little our believing will be continuously eroded by our environment. If, however, the Word so lives in individuals that what they produce is vivacious with that Word and if they produce for believers the things needed for their surroundings, then believing will constantly be increasing.

The Mystery was first revealed in the first century to the Apostle Paul, but apparently it did not become so embedded in God's people that all their surroundings, life-style, culture and art magnified and increased their believing in the Word.

To develop a culture, an entire culture, there must be a group of strong believers, a body working together. There was a group, a number, in the first century; but they had to spend their time fighting persecution, and consequently, could not spend their time developing skills in areas of culture. We shall see how peace and time both played important roles in allowing a Word-centered culture to develop in another era later on in this essay.

The first time the Mystery was given, it was not retained. The second time—today, in this ministry that stands for the rightly-divided Word—remember, the second time God does a thing it is established. That's us. We, here today, if the lord tarries, are on the threshold of developing a Word-centered culture. The road is clear. No one has done it yet in this Age of Grace. We have no limits. Our God is limitless in inspiration, ideas and power to carry it out. What a thrilling time to be alive! What a choice of activities, careers, specialties and professions lies before us! What multitudes of blessings are ready to fall into our hands, giving us the privilege of scattering them among God's people!

Let us then consider the possibilities of Word-centered culture. Remember, the Word will not emerge in the works of men's hands until it has absolutely prevailed in an individual's life at some point in time. Therefore, I cannot emphasize enough the importance of total commitment to the Word of God. It is exactly when a believer has relinquished every care and tie to his worldly interests and commits himself solely to that Word, that God Himself begins to open doors in that person's life for him to develop his abilities and to share his talents and skills with other believers.

In Proverbs 18:16 is written: "A man's gift maketh room for him, and bringeth him before great men." God never wastes anything, for He knows all things. He can always utilize an ability or talent in a committed believer. But if that believer is too devoted to his talent to release it for the love of God, the Word will never be in his works anyway.

God has provided each of us with a body and a soul and has put His spirit within. Each one is for our use and can be developed to bless God's people. As God put Adam in the garden "to dress it and to keep it," so we also are stewards of our bodies, our souls and our spirits. We can use them or we can squander them. If we do not use our bodies, muscles atrophy. If we do not use our minds and develop the lives of our souls, our minds and souls also atrophy.

With disuse our spirit, however, DOES NOT atrophy. That is God's great grace and mercy unto us.

Our spirits are eternal life. But, from neglect of our spiritual lives, we lose our ready source of power and inspiration. We quickly become those emaciated Christians that Dr. Wierwille talks about in the Power for Abundant Living class. The renewed mind is the key to power, and our walk before God consists of a daily balance of body, soul and spirit. The balance varies from individual believer to individual believer.

In this essay, since we are considering culture and the arts which are primarily the direct result of man's soul life, I shall be concentrating on the soul life. However, I am in no way suggesting that the body and the spirit are less important than the soul.

Now I would like to turn our thoughts to a few examples, both of individuals and whole cultures in the Word itself, before considering how these examples might be applied to us, the Body of Christ, today.

RICHNESS OF SOUL: TWO EXAMPLES

Culture flows out from the soul life, and I would first like to turn our attention to two individuals in God's Word that exhibited rich soul lives. There are many others, but one of my favorite examples of a rich and varied soul life and a great contributor to the culture of the time among God's people is King David. (For background read about him in II Samuel.) He is the only man that the Word calls "a man after God's own heart." What a compliment! What an honor!

How did David spend his life? When he was young, he was a shepherd. (Even today, some people's life's work is that of a shepherd—in Asia, the Middle East and Eastern Europe.) David was also a soldier. (How many people today make a career of the military?) David was also a king—which requires diplomacy, tact, organizational ability, decision-making ability, and administrative know-how for serving many people. (Might we not compare that position to the president of some worldwide corporation today? How many people today make their life's career as executives?) Already we see that David had much variety in his life.

But that is not all. He was also a dancer and a composer and a poet and a performer both of musical and poetic works. (How many people today make musical performance their life's work or have careers as singers of other people's compositions? How many people just compose or write for a living, but do not have it to perform before others? David did both: compose and perform.) He also went into the construction business— having prepared everything for the building of the Temple under his son Solomon.

Furthermore, David was a husband (of several wives), a father, a son, a lover and a friend. Granted, he did not do all the above-mentioned activities at one time. But in any case, he did not lead a one-sided life.

The beauty, variety and richness of his soul life and experience are reflected in the brilliance of the imagery in his psalms. When he speaks of the Lord as his shepherd, it is from firsthand experience. When he speaks of the enemy rising up, of smiting him, it is from firsthand experience on the battlefield. All his imagery comes right out of the guts of his life and experience. Granted, God inspired him, but these are David's words, David's vocabulary, which came from his own experiences.

But above all these things, he was consistently and faithfully a believer in the true and living God—even when he made mistakes. That is why the Word calls him "a man after God's own heart." His walk with God did not hinder him from becoming involved in life, from becoming an artist, from mastering certain areas of endeavor. In fact, I believe that it was his love for and belief in God that inspired him to lead such a rich, varied and exciting life, accomplishing so much in the senses realm. He thus made a great contribution to the culture of the time (as well as to subsequent generations of all those that read and believe the Word he wrote down). And God surely blessed the works of his mind and hands because these works blessed, inspired and built the believing of God's people in the true and living God.

Yet there is one greater than David—our lord and savior Jesus Christ, the Master himself. He is our greatest example. But wait, you may be thinking, Jesus never painted a picture. He never played a musical instrument. He never wrote a word (except perhaps on the ground in John chapter 8). He never designed a building, nor sculpted a sculpture. In fact, the Word says that he went around "doing good" and that his activities consisted of "teaching, preaching, and healing."

That is true. Even though he did none of the professional activities David so agilely performed, we know from the records in the Word that he was a keen observer of all life around him. And not only an observer, but the understanding he exhibits in many areas of life indicates that he might have had some firsthand experience in these areas also. He speaks in detail of agriculture, of the habits of animals, of many areas of nature, of trees and plants, the weather, of fishing, of building, of the military, and most keenly, he knew people, their hearts. By his words and actions, he was the greatest teacher of the human mind, the greatest healer of the human heart and a master of all phases of human relations.

True, Jesus Christ cannot be stereotyped into one or several professions as we think of professions today, for he had a greater field to master. He was the greatest artist, the only artist and master of life—all of life. He alone reached the highest degree of self-discipline and accomplishment—the perfect walk with God. His masterpiece was—and still is—his life. He mastered life, all of it, so that we today can have that source of unlimited power and energy as well as the written example of his walk.

Having mastered life, he made available to us the power to excel. Today we are his Body. Though we are *not* of the world, we nevertheless live *in* it. The masterpiece of Jesus Christ's life gives us the ability to excel in every or any area of life. He did not dictate a particular occupation or profession for us to go into. No, he mastered all of life so that we today can excel in any endeavor in this world, thus enabling us all to work together as one Body according to God's eternal purpose.

GOD'S STANDARD OF EXCELLENCE

Because we live in this world, we all need to do something (''if any would not work, neither should he eat"). In the great variety of talents, abilities and desires in the one Body, we all have ample opportunity to do things for others, as well as have things done for us. We need each other and we need things to do for each other. What are all these "things done" for each other but the sum and total of culture?

This spring I went to Ira Hearne at Way Farm #2 to inquire how to plant my garden. Mr. Hearne has been in charge of organic gardening for The Way International. He took considerable time and effort to provide me with materials and background information for my project. When I thanked him, he answered very simply: "I like to read your articles in the magazine. If you spent all your time learning and building experience in gardening, you would have no time to write. But this is what I do in the Body, so that other people can do other things. Because you write, I do not need to write, but I still have something to read."

What are gardening and writing but areas of culture? As we develop our abilities, talents, interests, we have something very important to contribute to the Body. And others, as they develop their expertise in other areas, have something very important and necessary to contribute to us.

What then is the standard of performance the true God sets before His people? It is stated in II Peter 1:3: "According as his divine power hath given unto us all things that *pertain* unto life and godliness, through the knowledge of him that hath called us to glory and [here it is!] virtue."

"Virtue", the Greek word *aretē*, is a unique and separated superiority in an excellent way, or excelling excellence. Our God has called us to excelling excellence! Excellence is our God's standard for His people; excellence is available. We can all walk toward God's excellence by applying His infallible principles in any area of human endeavor—believing (disciplined action, practice), faithfully (over a period of time) and constantly recognizing and improving on details.

Yes, our God sets before us a standard of superior excellence. Furthermore, through His Son Jesus Christ, He gives us power to work it and walk toward that goal. What a God!

THE BUILDING OF THE TABERNACLE

Now I would like to share with you from the Word two eras when there was a Word-centered culture.

In the days of Moses, after the children of Israel had been delivered out of the bondage of Egypt, they were together as a group, set apart from the surrounding unbelievers. They had a strong leader, Moses—a man of remarkable vision.

God commanded Moses to build a tabernacle which would be His habitation. Of course, we know that God fills the heavens and the earth, so He is not going to fit into a little tent or building. Why then a tabernacle? Because God's people were body and soul. They needed something to look at, to gather around, to concentrate upon in the senses realm, something that would turn their attention toward God and also build their believing in His presence.

No one at that time was closer to God than Moses, the man of God. Yet, although God gave him the commandment and *all* the details of carrying it out, Moses himself did not do the building. Many of God's people contributed and some in very special capacities. (To get the whole picture, reread the first five books of the Bible, especially in regards to the tabernacle, Exodus 25-40.)

In Exodus, God gives Moses the commandment to build the tabernacle.

Exodus 25:8 and 9:
And let them make me a sanctuary; that I may dwell among them.
According to all that I shew thee, *after* the pattern of the tabernacle, and the pattern of all the instruments thereof, even so shall ye make *it*.

Very noteworthy in the following several chapters is the minute detail with which God revealed the building of the tabernacle to Moses. EVERYTHING is covered—size, weight and materials for everything, as well as clothes (down to color, texture, combinations), even to the priests' blue shoelaces and also the curtain rings (number and exact size). These are only a few examples. The details in this section are so profuse that it would be necessary to quote the rest of the book. The point to see is that God gave a full and detailed vision of the final product, as well as the how of doing it, plus full details of all the activities to take place there.

Now, has God changed since the days of Moses in His willingness or His ability to provide necessary inspiration to His people to make something in this world that would bless His people?

Furthermore in Exodus 31 we read:
Exodus 31:1-3:
And the Lord spake unto Moses, saying,

See, I have called by name Bezaleel the son of Uri, the son
of Hur, of the tribe of Judah:
And I have filled him with the spirit of God, in wisdom,
and in understanding, and in knowledge, and in all manner of workmanship.

God continues to tell all these things to Moses and
then in Exodus 35, Moses recounts what God told him
to the children of Israel.

Exodus 35:30-35:
And Moses said unto the children of Israel,
See, the Lord hath called by name Bezaleel the son of Uri,
the son of Hur, of the tribe of Judah;
And he hath filled him with the spirit of God, in wisdom,
in understanding, and in knowledge, and in all manner of
workmanship;
And to devise curious works, to work in gold, and in
silver, and in brass,
And in the cutting of stones, to set *them*, and in carving of
wood, to make any manner of cunning work.
And he hath put in his heart that he may teach, *both* he,
and Aholiab, the son of Ahisamach, of the tribe of Dan.
Them hath he filled with wisdom of heart, to work all
manner of work, of the engraver, and of the cunning
workman, and of the embroiderer, in blue, and in purple,
in scarlet, and in fine linen, and of the weaver, *even* of
them that do any work, and of those that devise cunning
work.

Notice in verse 34, "that he may teach" all these
arts, crafts, skills. You see, they are not something one
is born with. These skills can be taught and they can be
learned; otherwise, God would not have put it in this
man's heart to teach them. These skills can be taught
and learned because they are a matter of principle, as I

discussed in the technical area in a preceding section.

Notice also that God inspired particular people to do the work. Is He not able to inspire individual believers today to perform works that will bless the Body of Christ as they walk in alignment and harmony with Him, be it in designing a house, writing a song, a poem, a play or designing a line of edifying clothing? Has God run out of ideas?

THE THREE HEARTS OF EXODUS 35

There is something further I want to bring to your attention in Exodus 35. There are three ''hearts'' in this section discussing the people who contributed to the building of the tabernacle.

The first is a willing heart. People had to contribute from a willing heart. They had to want to do it, want to do it for God and His glory. As it says in Exodus 35:5: ''Take ye from among you an offering unto the Lord: whosoever *is* of a willing heart, let him bring it, an offering of the Lord. . . .'' First of all, the people had to give their goods and services out of a willing heart, out of the love of God.

Secondly, God called the wise-hearted. Exodus 35:10: ''And every wise hearted among you shall come, and make all that the Lord hath commanded. . . .'' Now, what is wisdom? Wisdom is knowledge applied, or more specifically, the application of knowledge to its best purposes. Wisdom is know-how. To have know-how someone must be practiced in an area. You see, God did not just pull Joe Believer off the street and say: ''You are going to be an engraver (or a stone cutter or a weaver or an embroiderer).'' No, that would have been in the category of possession. God asked for wise-hearted people. They already had knowledge in their fields. Not only did they have knowledge, but they had practiced already (wisdom). They were already skilled craftsmen, artisans, artists and workers. They were professionals already. (Remember the framework: spiritual, technical, opinion? There it is!) These people loved God first, were spiritually right on, and they also had a high degree of technical proficiency. They were, wise-hearted.

How did they get wise-hearted? The same way we do today. At some point someone makes a decision to go into a particular field. (In those days professions were most often passed down from father to son.) Then he probably goes to work as a student apprentice with experienced people. Then comes believing, disciplined action, faithfulness, practice, improvement and the concomitant mastery over details until he becomes a wise-hearted master of his craft. To be wise-hearted, those people in Exodus 35 must have worked toward that excellence—and they did not even have Christ in them!

Once the people had a willing heart and a wise heart, they were in a position for the third heart.

Exodus 35:21:
And they came, every one whose heart stirred him up, and every one whom his spirit made willing, *and* they brought the Lord's offering to the work of the tabernacle of the congregation, and for all his service, and for the holy garments.

Exodus 36:2:
And Moses called Bezaleel and Aholiab, and every wise

hearted man, in whose heart the Lord had put wisdom, *even* every one whose heart stirred him up to come unto the work to do it.

There it is—the stirred heart. Once they were willing and wise, God could stir up their hearts so they would do it, bring the work into evidence, carry it out, accomplish it. They were stirred to carve that stone, to embroider, to weave, to work gold and silver, to engrave, to bring to pass whatever needed to be done to complete that tabernacle as a beautiful, inspiring, worthy habitation for the true and living God. Isn't that wonderful?

I believe God has not changed. In fact, I believe that "more, quicker, better" works are available today in this administration of the one Body with Christ living within each believer.

As in those days, our first and total commitment must be to God and His Word. Then He will open doors for us to develop skill in all areas of life—so that we also can become wise-hearted in our fields. Then, God can and will STIR our hearts as needs arise in the Body to bring great works to pass which will glorify Him and build the believing of His people.

THE BUILDING OF THE TEMPLE

Lest you think that the above was all a special favor to Moses, the man of God, let me bring your attention to a second example of a magnificent Word-centered culture. This was during the time of David and Solomon. At this time God commanded that a temple be built for His habitation. A temple was more permanent than the tabernacle which was portable.

Significantly, Solomon had peace all around. I Kings

5:4 states: "But now the Lord my God hath given me rest on every side, *so that there is* neither adversary nor evil occurrent."

Rest on every side gave people time to develop skills for this tremendous undertaking—the building of the Temple—as they did not need to be soldiers in the battlefield.

Although David was commanded to plan for the Temple, God did not have him to build it, but put the actual building in the hands of Solomon, David's son. Nevertheless, God gave David the plan. In I Chronicles, David addresses Solomon thus:

> I Chronicles 28:10-12:
> Take heed now; for the Lord hath chosen thee to build an house for the sanctuary: be strong, and do *it*.
> Then David gave to Solomon his son the pattern of the porch, and of the houses thereof, and of the treasuries thereof, and of the upper chambers thereof, and of the inner parlours thereof, and of the place of the mercy seat,
> And the pattern of all that he had by the spirit, of the courts of the house of the Lord, and of all the chambers round about, of the treasuries of the house of God, and of the treasuries of the dedicated things.

He continues here to enumerate the details. (You can read more details of the Temple in I Kings 5—7.) And in I Chronicles 28:19, David tells exactly how he got the plan. "All *this*, *said David*, the Lord made me understand in writing by *his* hand upon me, *even* all the works of this pattern."

Look at this! God gave David a full and detailed blueprint with all the works of the pattern. God left nothing to chance, but gave David every detail down to the weights of the candlesticks and of the curtain hooks.

I Chronicles 28:20:
And David said to Solomon his son,
Be strong and of good courage, and do *it*:
Fear not, nor be dismayed: for the Lord God, *even* my God, *will be* with thee; he will not fail thee, nor forsake thee, until thou hast finished all the work for the service of the house of the Lord.

What a wonderful exhortation from father to son! God wanted this work to be completed, to be a beautiful and glorious work which would inspire and edify His people.

Consider the matter: where does man derive inspiration? From his surroundings or directly from the spirit—one or the other. How many gorgeous, right-on, glory-to-God buildings were around in those days? None. There were temples of the heathen, the unbelievers—some of them pretty impressive, still standing today—but who inspires the unbelievers? Not the true and living God. They are not listening to Him.

How wonderful of God. He did not say to David: "Build me a grand and glorious temple" and then leave David to figure out the details, because then David would have had to look to the works of the unbelievers to show him how. No, God is wise.

For we are so lost when left to our own devices. Man alone stumbles, wanders and falls. God is wise—wise and wonderful. He knew what would be edifying to His people, what would bring glory to Him, and He gave David every minute detail and the instruction of the pattern so there could be no confusion, no doubt, no misunderstandings.

David received all this information because he was in touch with God. That is surely a key. And if we look closer, we will see that it was not only the Temple that was inspired by God, but that the culture of the time was Word-centered and unbelievably splendid.

We have the record of an outsider's reaction to this Word-centered culture.

I Kings 10:1 and 2:
And when the queen of Sheba heard of the fame of Solomon concerning the name of the Lord, she came to prove him with hard questions.
And she came to Jerusalem with a very great train, with camels that bare spices, and very much gold, and precious stones: and when she was come to Solomon, she communed with him of all that was in her heart.

We see that the queen of Sheba was no slouch. She must have had quite a "queendom," quite a culture herself, with mining (gold, precious stones), industry, trade, agriculture (spices). She had livestock, servants—a great train. She must have had a few impressive things going for herself in Sheba.

I Kings 10:4 and 5:
And when the queen of Sheba had seen all Solomon's wisdom, and the house that he had built,
And the meat of his table, and the sitting of his servants, and the attendance of his ministers, and their apparel, and his cupbearers, and his ascent by which he went up unto the house of the Lord; there was no more spirit in her.

Look at this! The Word, the living Word, so permeated all areas of people's activities, even those of the servants. Believers cooked, prepared and served those meals. Believers designed the clothes. Believers built the Temple, did the artwork, the gold and silver work, the decoration. The living Word was in evidence in every area of human behavior. As is written in I Chronicles 29:25a: "And the Lord magnified Solomon exceedingly in the sight of all Israel."

The queen of Sheba could not believe what she saw! Her words reflect her amazement and admiration.

I Kings 10:6-8:
And she said to the king, It was a true report that I heard in mine own land of thy acts and of thy wisdom.
Howbeit, I believed not the words, until I came, and mine eyes had seen *it*: and, behold, the half was not told me: thy wisdom and prosperity exceedeth the fame which I heard.
Happy *are* thy men, happy *are* these thy servants, which stand continually before thee, *and* that hear thy wisdom.

What was Solomon's wisdom at that time but the Word of God? That was the basis on which every activity was carried out.

What a record! The queen of Sheba had never seen anything like the culture of Solomon, and we know she lived in quite a culture herself in Sheba, for in verse 10 are recorded magnificent and sophisticated gifts she gave to Solomon. Yet, the culture, the Word-centered culture of Solomon's day, overwhelmed her with its unparalleled magnificence.

Both David and Solomon grew up under the ministry of Samuel the prophet. During his day the Word really began to live again as it had not lived since the days of Joshua.

Let us review briefly a few of the factors which preceded the blooming of a Word-centered culture at that time. Samuel was a strong leader, and we know he had a school of the prophets so that there was leadership trained in the Word. He annointed Saul, during whose reign there were wars with the surrounding unbelievers, the Philistines. However, under David's rule, the land was recaptured, authority secured and order restored; moreover, the Word was living in the king and in the leadership.

By the time Solomon came to the throne, there was peace, and there was time to build trained leadership. For the culture to flourish as it did in those days, it took time for the Word to permeate the society via the trained spiritual leadership; and there was time also for people to develop skills in all the arts, crafts and workmanship required to make the Word live so dynamically in all areas of man's accomplishments.

I cannot imagine in detail the songs they sang, the clothes they wore, the architecture, the manners, the industry, the splendor. But I know it happened. Word-centered culture flourished at that time. Word-centered culture can flourish today.

WHAT IS AVAILABLE TODAY

With this ministry today there is a man of vision, a strong leader committed to teaching the accuracy and integrity of the Word of God. There is also concerted effort to train and build leadership (through the WOW and Way Corps programs) so that the rightly-divided Word can spread throughout the body of believers.

And right now, we have peace—right now there is time to develop skills, to practice, to experience and to develop ourselves.

Now I ask you again: has God changed since the days of David and Solomon? Has He forgotten that we need to be told every detail? If He would do that in David's day to help bring into evidence a great and glorious building and a whole culture that would build believing in Him, would He not do the same and more for us, His sons, today?

God knows we live in the world. He knows we have material things about us. Remember, everything in evidence to the senses either builds believing or tears it down in either obvious or subtle ways. Would not God want us to be surrounded by edifying things: wearing sharp, edifying clothing; hearing inspiring, edifying music; eating healthy food; seeing inspiring, edifying productions on TV, at the theater, the movies, the opera; reading edifying poetry, novels; living in inspiring, light, edifying dwellings, with inspiring paintings or photos on the walls?

And would He not also be able and willing to inspire His people and give them minute, beautiful details and ideas in music, painting, writing, clothes, interior decorating, architecture, construction, etc.? Could not He do that today for His people as He did for Moses and for David and for Solomon (as well as many others in the Word)?

I believe that He can. He has already started. We have Way Productions building that excellence in music. We have Way Builders. We have budding writers. We have Reflections for our personal appearance. And there are more and more believers in professions: doctors, educators, farmers, businessmen—people in all walks of life committed to the Word.

Yes, we today are standing at the threshold of a Word-centered culture. Today, we are His habitation.

Ephesians 2:19-22:
Now therefore ye are no more strangers and foreigners, but fellowcitizens with the saints, and of the household of God;
And are built upon the foundation of the apostles and prophets, Jesus Christ himself being the chief corner *stone*;
In whom all the building fitly framed together groweth unto an holy temple in the Lord:
In whom ye also are builded together for an habitation of God through the Spirit.

We ourselves are His permanent dwelling place in this administration. We are the temple of the living God with God in Christ in us.

Look at the minute attention God paid to each individual part of the tabernacle and to every corner of the Temple. He cared for every shoelace of the priests, for every curtain hook, for every stone and how it was engraved and placed on the priest's robe. Should not God also have placed each one of us in the Body with at least as much care, concern and interest? What a completely open field! What infinite possibilities in every area of human endeavor! All the doors are open. We have seen nothing like it in our lifetime. The fullness of Word-centered culture has not yet been realized in this Administration of Grace. God is ready. He waits upon us to rise up and believe.

I can see turning on the TV and tuning in Word-centered programs. Perhaps the records of David or

Abraham, or the Book of Acts in half-hour segments soap-opera style. (Instead of "As the World Turns" we have "As the Word Turns.") I can see theater productions right from the accuracy and integrity of the Word. I would love to buy clothes made by believers, designed to bring out the Christ in me. I can see paintings on my walls by believers—painted with the love of God and executed with breathtaking skill and artistry. And I would love to have furniture designed and made by believers.

Who knows? Perhaps God has some ideas for furniture design that no one in the world has thought of yet. Perhaps He knows of musical instruments that have not been invented yet; transportation not yet dreamed of; buildings never before thought of; oratorios, operas, songs never imagined—all that would bring glory to Him and build believing among His people.

Yes, and there are Limb coordinators also, and Branch coordinators, and Twig coordinators. There are also prophets, apostles, teachers, evangelists, and pastors, governments and helps. There is more than enough for everyone to do. Our God is rich, whether in the quality of our spiritual lives or in the richness and beauty of our soul lives.

I know one thing—I shall not be able to do all of the above. Neither will you. I may do one thing; you may concentrate upon another. Someone else may do something else. Yes, we are a body, one Body. We need each other. We are all called and placed in that Body as it has pleased God, our Father.

Wherever we are in the Body, whatever we do, I cannot stress enough the singular importance of the Word, the Word, THE WORD in each of our daily lives. And daily does not mean all day (although that might not hurt once in awhile). As I shared with you in the beginning of this essay, I once thought that daily meant all day—that God's will for me was that I sit in an unassuming corner, in some unassuming attire, and read, study and work the Word all day, only leaving to attend fellowships every evening. I thank God that my vision of the walk before Him has increased and has taken on a more abundant texture, color and dimension.

If we are in the Word daily and apply God's Word to whatever we do, wherever we go, we can meditate on God's Word, speak in tongues and allow God to teach us. It matters not whether we are a student in drama school, performing surgery, president of a corporation, a fisherman, a farmer, an engineer, an auto mechanic or a poet. We can still excel in one of the above areas and also participate in Twigs—as leaf or coordinator.

In no other way will the Word evidence itself in Word-centered culture unless it prevails daily and grows in each of our individual lives. By prevailing and growing in our lives, that Word releases in us the unlimited power to excel in any area of endeavor. Today, we can build excellence, bless others and be blessed.

A challenge is to be pitted toe to toe, face to face, nose to nose, eyeball to eyeball with what is available. We stand on the threshold today of Word-centered culture according to our believing. It is available. How big do we dare to believe?

Essay Three

Thinking Through Words

In the opening essay of this series, I have sought to inspire the mind, to expand vision. In a few words a mental appetizer was presented. In the second essay, I have set the foundation of culture and the arts from the Word of God, shown examples of Word-centered culture in the Word and suggested possible avenues of its application today in this Administration of Grace.

In the third and last essay of this series on the theme of Word-centered culture, I shall be rethinking with you certain specific words and ideas that apply to culture. These are words that I used for years with a worldly understanding. But only since my study of God's Word have these words become clear, meaningful and really useful to me. Our thinking, our dreams, our visions, our ideals and goals can never be greater than our vocabulary. As our understanding of words increases in variety and depth, our dreams and visions can expand, and therefore our accomplishments can increase in detail and excellence.

Often we tend not to think too carefully of the meaning of words we use. But because God says what He means and means what He says, and He is our Number One example of communicating, I have begun to devote more and more time to thinking through word meanings and usages. Since I use these words, I desire to know to the best of my understanding exactly what they mean. Thinking through the words I shall handle here in the area of culture has helped me to clarify my thoughts and increase my understanding of God and His Word. I believe it may stimulate your thinking also.

Many times I hear the words *expression* and *communication* used interchangeably. Sometimes they can be correctly substituted for one another. However, there is a very important difference.

EXPRESSION AND COMMUNICATION

Expression is a one-way street; communication, a two-way street. A communication must be received to be a communication. Until it is received, it remains an expression. As a simple example, I could express myself to you in French. If you do not understand French, I will have communicated nothing to you (except that I am making sounds).

Now, it is possible to express oneself and also to communicate something. However, just because one has expressed himself does not necessarily mean he has communicated.

In I Corinthians 14:19 we have a fine example of the

difference. Paul says: "Yet in the church [among the believers] I had rather speak five words with my understanding, that *by my voice* I might teach others also, than ten thousand words in an *unknown* tongue."

Paul is here concerned with communication. If he speaks in tongues, he is communicating with God, he is expressing prayer and praise to God. But speaking in tongues aloud, he would be communicating nothing to others. Communication is one of the greatest principles of the Word and the world—giving and receiving.

Remember, a message must be received to be a communication. Until it is received it is an expression.

Now, let us turn to two other words: *form* and *content*. Content is *something*. However, there is no way to communicate content unless it is in some form or another.

Furthermore, without light there can be no form.

Now, God in the beginning (Genesis 1:1) had a desire, a purpose, a will. He moved. He created the heavens and the earth (forms). In the second verse of Genesis 1, darkness came upon His creation for we read: "And [But] the earth was [became] without form, and void; and darkness *was* upon the face of the deep. And the Spirit of God moved upon the face of the waters." You see, without light there can be no form and therefore no communication.

To give order, God's first words were: "Let there be light." With light there can be form again, and if there is form, there can be communication—giving and receiving. God continues to speak into being: the firmament and waters, waters and land; then grass, herbs and trees; then lights in the firmaments—the sun, the moon and the stars; then moving creatures—in the water, in the air and on the land.

Look at this—do you see a pattern? He moved from immense, general forms to more minute, detailed and specific forms.

It is the sixth day. Has God communicated anything yet? No. Why not? Because up to now none of these *forms* could receive. He has expressed Himself from the grand-scale forms down to the smaller forms, but no one was there to receive God's expressions.

The entire creation was the immense and perfect setting for the desire of God's heart—someone to receive, someone He could both express and communicate Himself to. God wanted a family, wanted fellowship, someone to share Himself with, someone to bless, someone who could receive His blessings. So on the sixth day, God formed, made and created man in His own image and likeness— someone with whom He, God, could communicate, someone with whom He, God, could have fellowship, warm and intimate, Father to son.

From that point on His whole creation was no longer a mere *expression* of Himself, of His power, His ingenuity, His ability, His imagination, but a multitude of forms that *communicated* Himself (the greatest content) to man.

This is plainly stated in Romans 1:20: "For the invisible things of him [God] from the creation of the world are clearly seen, being understood by the things that are made, *even* his eternal power and Godhead; so that they are without excuse."

So God *expressed* Himself in the entire creation and

He expressed Himself also in making man. Furthermore, in making man able to receive from God personally and directly, God could now *communicate*, for that is His heart's desire—to share Himself.

Well, we all know what happened. Adam lost his connection with God, that is, his spiritual "content," and God continued throughout history to reestablish His communication (*logos*) on an even firmer basis. And He did. God perfected His communication to man in Jesus Christ by all that God accomplished for us in Christ Jesus. God made available the new birth which is incorruptible, eternal and unconditional—a perfect communication.

CONTENT AND FORM

We have received. We speak in tongues. We have received and we know it and can be eternally thankful by praising God constantly in perfect prayer—giving thanks well. That solid knowledge which we have received makes us able also to pass on the treasure, the greatest content. For it says in II Corinthians 4:7: "But we have this treasure [content] in earthen vessels [forms], that the excellency of the power may be of God, and not of us."

One conclusion we might draw is that form is valueless without content. We have all read a beautiful poem, seen a painting, heard a song beautifully performed. These might have had fine forms, yet without content (message, *logos*) they are nothing— empty expressions. Or, perhaps we know a person—beautiful to look at in body and soul—BUT, without the content of the treasure, God in Christ, that person is nothing more than a temporarily animated pile of dust.

Therefore, one might conclude, form is just dust. Content is everything. But wait, let us turn this around. Where would the Christ-in-you be without your body and soul? Somewhere with God. Wonderful. But then, God could not be communicating to others without your form, your body and soul for His spirit to dwell in. Suddenly, the body and soul become very important, for without them God cannot communicate and that is God's heart's desire—to give and to be received—to have fellowship.

Truly God's heart is for and with His people. Therefore, *form* takes on a new importance, a new dimension in our eyes. We see that form is empty without content, but once the content—the treasure—is there, form becomes very, very important, even in everyday life.

God exhorts us to be followers or imitators of Him (Ephesians 5:1). And did not He pay great attention to the details of His forms? Consider the plant kingdom or the animal kingdom. Why, just among beetles and butterflies, there is an amazing variety in color, size and features. These are merely two kinds of insects. How careful God was, how precise, how various in the multitudes of things He made. And if God gave much attention and care to the forms of these creatures, how about man?

Most of us have two eyes, a nose, a mouth, two arms, two legs, and yet, bodies are so incredibly different. No two people really look alike physically. How about in the soul life, in personality? If there is such variety in body, surely there must be a tremendous variety in soul life—in interests, talents, abilities, capabilities, inclinations, yearnings. And of course, there is. God made us that way.

Now, consider the Body of Christ in this Age of Grace. How wonderful to have this variety in the Body, for there is room for those who desire to build, to paint, to write, to play music, to sing, to coordinate, to organize, to teach, to minister and on and on. There is room for each one to develop himself to his fullest potential and each person's abilities make room for him. If God paid such careful attention to the forms of His expression and communication, how about us in our daily activities, in the things we do and make? Our lives manifest a multitude of forms—how we look on the outside, how we speak, how we carry ourselves, how we care for our surroundings—these are all forms in which we participate just by living.

Taking God as our example, what kind of attention to detail might we pay to the forms in our lives? The more the eyes of our understanding are enlightened to the greatness, the magnificence of the treasure within each of us, the more we become interested in imitating God, in paying attention to minute details in every form of our activities. For he who is faithful in details is much more likely to be faithful in grand endeavors. Our attention to the details on the outside is in direct proportion to our understanding of the greatness of the treasure on the inside.

So many of us, when we first heard the Word and learned that God looked upon our hearts and that our hearts are right before Him, flung everything to the winds. I did—what did it matter what people thought, or how I looked, or what I wore, or how I spoke? What did it matter if I misspelled or mispronounced words, or wrote sloppily? What did it matter if I talked everyone's ear off, if I cleaned the house or not? What did it all matter? After all, God was looking at my heart. And my heart was right before Him; after all, Christ was living there.

I relished this, my new-found freedom, to cast aside my previous lifelong bondage to all my physical surroundings. Suddenly, I did not need to pay attention to anything. I was righteous no matter what I did or did not do. It took me a little while to realize that I had overlooked something of immense importance. Perhaps some of you reading this will recognize these circumstances.

The more I delved into the Word and the more I desired God to be my example, the more I desired to do everything the best I possibly could—to think things through, to pay attention to details, to plan. This approach is not new; it was simply very new to me—to see more and more of my activities in the light of my growing knowledge of His Word. Even Jesus said:

Luke 14:28-30:
For which of you, intending to build a tower, sitteth not down first, and counteth the cost, whether he have *sufficient* to finish *it*?
Lest haply, after he hath laid the foundation, and is not able to finish *it*, all that behold *it* begin to mock him,
Saying, This man began to build, and was not able to finish.

Because of the greatness of God and the greatness of His power in Christ in us, we can now become vitally

THINKING THROUGH WORDS / 67

aware of form, persistent in detail and faithful in carrying out any project among our numerous activities.

God's purpose was and still is to communicate. (Jesus Christ is the *logos* in person; the Bible is the *logos* in writing. Both are God's communication of Himself to man.) Therefore, if we desire to do God's will and imitate Him, our purpose also is to communicate. God also expressed Himself, and the Christ in each one of us frees us to express fully our best selves, the fullness of our abilities and talents—BUT, to the end that we communicate to others the knowledge of God, so that they receive and can communicate to others.

We communicate our knowledge of God through various forms. And now we are right back to culture and the arts—which are none other than forms of expression and communication, giving and receiving in the one Body of Christ.

For example, music is one medium of expression and communication, but within that medium, or form, there are quite a number of specific forms: song (with or without accompaniment), small group (Joyful Noise, a family), choir, choral works, oratorio, opera, musical comedy, instrumental (solo, duet, trio, quartet, etc.), symphony, concerto. These are all specific forms in which music can be communicated. If I were involved in music, I would want to have thought through these forms, investigated their potential, to understand more fully my media and materials.

Written words or literature, a second example, is another medium of expression and communication. But, within the written form there are many more specific forms: poetry, novel, essay, drama, journalism, biography, parable, prose, autobiography, research writing, to name a few. For this series of thoughts on culture, I chose the *essay* form, rather than poetry, journalism or drama. I chose the essay form because it was the best form within which to develop these ideas on culture, so that you would have the best advantage to follow and understand. To choose the essay form, I had to know something about forms of the written word and what each one could best accomplish.

Every particular form has certain advantages and disadvangates in communication. We need to pay attention to audience, occasion, mood, need and other circumstances to choose the best forms. Within any area of arts and culture it is a great help to know the potential of the forms available to us. This means we need to prove, to utilize, to experiment. Wisdom is knowledge applied—know-how. If God gave so much care and attention to the minute details of forms He developed, should not we also study, work, practice, distinguish and care for forms also in the things we produce?

It has been said: "Man cannot control something that he cannot define, and he cannot manage a thing he cannot control." Before we work with something, we must first define it. Defining something has to do with the recognition and study of form. First, we need to see and isolate the form. Then, we can begin to handle it, learn to control it, see its potential, its limitations. When we have learned control of that form, we can then manage it thoroughly. (I am here restating from the second essay the process of technical development from less skillful to more skillful.)

Now that we understand expression and communication, form and content, let me trace deeper a thought from the previous section. I stated that traditionally the so-called "fine arts," or "creative arts," including painting, sculpture, architecture, literature, music and perhaps also theater and dance, have been exalted, while other human activities are minimized. I stated that there are no "better" or "superior" areas of culture. But I believe that what is best is what is needed at the time.

Now, however, I am going to turn around and contradict myself! Watch it. I am going to say now that the list of human activities in the above paragraph IS BETTER; it is superior in a certain framework of reference. There is a great truth behind this worldly myth, and it is important that we see and understand it.

From the point of view of the giver, the producer, the doer, the maker of something, there is no better person or ability. Someone may have invested much of his life in knitting, have become an artist, a master in this area, and someone else may have invested his life in architecture. Each of these people might produce a masterpiece in his particular specialty.

God alone is the judge as to whether each one did his best or fell short of what he was capable. Each person receives as he gives in whatever he does—the joy is in the labor itself. As Ecclesiastes 2:24 states: "*There is* nothing better for a man, *than* that he should eat and drink, and *that* he should make his soul enjoy good in his labour. This also I saw, that it *was* from the hand of God."

Then what is the difference? The difference lies in

the receiving end, not in the giving end. Certain forms of human activity in culture have a *greater potential for communication*. Certain forms can potentially reach and stir more people.

There is nothing left today of Jesus' seamless robe for which the soldiers cast lots. But there are buildings that have stood for over 2,000 years and which today communicate to us the culture of that time. From the building we can see the dreams, visions and ideals of those people. We can see what tools they used, how they did things, their ingenuity, their imagination, their systems of value. Through that building, a culture of ancient times still communicates to us today. There is a greater potential to reach more people through certain media of expression and communication—that is why these forms are greater. That is why these forms need to be emphasized and encouraged.

What remnants do we have of past civilizations, past cultures, that communicate to us today? Architecture, sculpture, painting, music and literature—written words—and this last is the greatest form of communication.

That is why God had a book written, for the written Word can potentially communicate with precision to the greatest number of people over time and space. Words are the most specific form of communication. Even though they are still at times misunderstood, they have the greatest potential to reach others to the end that people receive and understand.

You see, God did not have a painting painted or a building built, and say: "Whenever people see this picture or walk into this building, they will believe, they will understand.'' These forms are not specific enough. If I were unlearned and saw a painting of a handsome man by a rock, coming out of a hole in the ground looking pleased, I could not be born again, unless someone spoke to me or showed me words to explain Romans 10:9. The only way to be born again today is through believing the specific words of Romans 10:9.

Now, a beautiful picture might help me better visualize the event. A building might help put me in the mood. Music might set me at ease, relax me, but I would still need the specific words, the accurate words, to have the optimum opportunity to receive.

I am not here suggesting that everything but the Word, the written Word, is unimportant. I am endeavoring to set its importance. Man is a creature of many moods, many abilities, many activities, many needs and there is room for them all. We need to be aware of how the arts enhance and emphasize the prime importance of God's Word. We all love variety and change. We all move through a great variety of contexts in life, and every one of these contexts can be edifying, enriching.

When I first began dwelling on these thoughts and saw the supreme importance of God's Word, the written Word, I found myself wondering then about other forms of media, of communication. I saw how the written or spoken Word could be used in music, in songs where that Word was understood, but I did not understand the need for instrumental music. Because it had no words, I set it below vocal music in my mind.

At that time, I was working on an audiovisual presentation. The task was to put color slides to a sound track for the purpose of explaining one of the ministry's programs. At one point I saw the pictures with the spoken sound track. It was all good, but was so one-dimensional. It lacked color and texture and depth. I saw how important instrumental music was to that sound track. The audiovisual show without the music to emphasize, smooth and color it was difficult to receive. Later, however, with a musical score woven in, the whole show sprang to life. It was then that I reevaluated my temporary snubbing of instrumental music.

I enjoy films. Working on audiovisual presentations I began to dream of whole feature films, video programs that would build believing, build God's Word, be exciting, intricate, deep, worthy of thought, because they would be presenting some aspect of the more abundant life, some portion of God's Word. I began to think of what was involved and how important whole instrumental musical scores would be to the excellency of such films. Instrumental music does have a place, a very important place. There is a need in this area, as well as in all areas of life. I have digressed with this example to show that there is room for all abilities, all forms of communication, but that all must be to the end of communicating God's Word.

The written Word is the most effective, the most expedient. The greatest of ideas of all times have been transmitted to other people in writing.

Today, however, tapes are being used effectively; film is great; video is great. Praise God for them. Since they are available today, we can use them to communicate God's Word to people. But the paraphernalia involved—equipment, electricity, replacement parts, etc.—is expensive. Compared to all that, a book is small, can contain so much, is easily carried, requires little care, in fact, requires nothing—all it requires is that it be read.

When Jesus Christ lived on earth, his life blessed many people. He had great influence in his immediate surroundings. Yet the only reason we know that today is because of God's Word. Because it was written, the life of Christ is known and has impact today, 2,000 years later. Today, through the written Word, we are in his presence as though he himself walked among us. Spoken words die with the speaker, but if the words are written, they can reach people across centuries of time and miles of space.

Therefore, we see the truth behind the worldly assertion that the arts are superior. The error lies in the worldly conclusion that because the arts are effective in communicating ideas, the people who do them are somehow superior. But we can see from the above discussion that from the giving standpoint there is no difference in human activities. In the Body of Christ today, every ability is needed. Any ability can be developed, and each person receives according to his giving of his time and energy.

However, from the receiving point of view, certain forms of expression and communication are more far-reaching and can have a greater influence. Because God's desire is to reach people, to share Himself, certain forms are to be encouraged because they have a wider reach and more direct effect. And these forms are those generally called the fine arts.

CREATIVITY AND STEWARDSHIP

In this final segment on Word-centered culture, I would like to handle another pair of words in the area of culture: *creativity* and *plagiarism*.

In the world, man's "creativity" is greatly cherished. We hear of the "creative arts," "creative expression," "creative thoughts." Creativity is the much-admired quality everyone wants to have. When someone is so-called creative, he puts his name to his works and anywhere he is quoted or referred to, there must be an asterisk (*) with a note saying: "So-and-so is the brilliant, original mind that thought this thing up." If no reference is given him, the originator of the thought, then that is plagiarism—the robbery of an idea, thought, words, without giving the originator credit. When and where there is creativity among men, there is also plagiarism, along with envy, strife, competitiveness, pride, boastfulness, self-adulation.

Now let us look at God's Word and His attitude. We know that creativity, which is the bringing into being something that never was, is God's prerogative. He is the *only* Creative One. In Ecclesiastes 1:9b it is written: "*There is* no new *thing* under the sun." Therefore, there is no way man can be creative—in no way can he bring into being something from nothing. He can utilize what is available and in his handling there is a wonderful newness to himself and those around him; but man cannot be genuinely creative.

The reason I am handling this word is that I have encountered believers who have set creativity as their goal, and when I have shared that creativity is God's privilege—not man's—these believers have suddenly felt there was nothing worth doing anymore, that all that was available, therefore, was lukewarm rehash.

Even I had a sense of loss *for a moment* when I realized that creativity or "creative writing" was not available to me as a goal. That sense of loss came over me because most of my life, being around the people I was around, creativity had been blown up in my mind as the only worthwhile activity.

When we are confronted by the great truths of the Word, we often need to rethink our former ideas, reorganize our minds, reorder our thought patterns and the words of our ideas according to these great truths. This is exactly what I share with you in this section—the reorganization of thoughts and the rethinking of certain words.

Let us look at God's attitude toward His Word. He says again and again: think it, remember it, say it, repeat it, do it, use it. He gives us His Word to be used. (There is no plagiarism.) In fact, God tells us to use ALL that He has created and given to us—our surroundings (land and materials) and our own abilities and talents.

What did you or I have to do with "making" our bodies? Nothing. We simply arrived with all the potential physical characteristics included. What did you or I have to do with "making" our minds, our souls? Not much. Most of our attitudes were formed by the time we were six. Later on in our lives, perhaps we made some decisions of pursuing certain interests and not others, but the basis of our mental values and attitudes was still formed very early in our lives by our heredity, as well as by the people and the things around us. What did you or I have to do with creating our spirit life within? You and I "believed unto" being born again. God did the miracle—He created eternal life seed within.

God brought to pass our bodies, souls and spirits and His exhortation to us is: use them, develop them, share them, abound unto all good works. We are stewards of our bodies, souls and spirits. We are stewards of our surroundings. We are stewards of God's Word! All the above God has formed, made and created for us to use, to develop, to share with others in many, many forms of expression and communication.

Stewardship is the wonderful and exciting relationship we have to all our surroundings, including ourselves—our bodies, souls and spirits. In this context let me call to your attention the parable of the talents in Matthew 25:14-29.

Matthew 25:14:
For *the kingdom of heaven is* as a man travelling into a far country, *who* called his own servants, and delivered unto them his goods.

Notice they were "his servants," his own people, and "his goods" that he delivered unto them.

Matthew 25:15:
And unto one he gave five talents, to another two, and to another one; to every man according to his several ability; and straightway took his journey.

The man gave of "his goods," but in giving them, the servants now had authority to control, to develop, to utilize them. Notice the man gave "to every man according to his several ability," not according to his person, but according to certain conditions.

The servant with the five talents "went and traded," invested and doubled. So did the servant that had two talents. He also doubled the talents allocated to him.

The two men who went and traded, gained. They both doubled. Now what was the master's (lord's) reaction to this?

Matthew 25:21:

His lord said unto him, Well done, *thou* good and faithful servant: thou hast been faithful over a few things, I will make thee ruler over many things: enter thou into the joy of thy lord.

In using what was given them by their lord, they not only doubled, but they also caused their lord joy.

Now, the third servant with the one talent, having buried it in the ground, explained to his returning lord: "And I was afraid, and went and hid thy talent in the earth..." (verse 25).

It is always fear that keeps us from acting, doing, using what we have. Fear keeps us from developing our potential that we have been given. The lord calls him a "wicked and slothful servant" for not utilizing what was given him. Thus, the lord takes the talent away from the servant and gives it to the one with ten.

Matthew 25:29:

For unto every one that hath shall be given, and he shall have abundance: but from him that hath not shall be taken away even that which he hath.

The great wisdom and exhortation here is to use what is given us, use it all for only then can we have abundance. There is only one way to receive anything— and that is to give. All we have to give is energy and time—physical (body), mental (soul) and spiritual

(Christ in you). The Christ in us enables us to go fearlessly into the deep, to cast out all our nets, to put forth the energy so that we may receive in abundance.

So what if we cannot be creative? There are numerous, wonderful things for us to do in life. Just because there is nothing new under the sun does not mean we need fall over and die. No, each one of us has the joy and privilege to experience the doing, the living and thereby to know (*ginōskō*—to know by experience) God even better.

A good example of what I am discussing here is childbirth. Now, there is nothing less creative or more common and universal than childbirth. Everyone of us went through it to get here. Just because it has been done billions of times throughout history, is that any reason not to have children?

Many of us will go through a childbirth (other than our own birth) closely involved in the situation as a mother or a father. Those of you who have already had children know that the birth of your own child is different from every other birth throughout history. It is intensely personal, overwhelmingly significant, deeply meaningful and vitally important. The experience has immense impact on your life and opens doors for learning you never considered. Even though childbirth is the most common, the most unoriginal, the most uncreative human activity, it has intense personal depth and learning to each individual person every time.

So what if there are no "creative" plots under the sun, no "creative" songs, no "creative" visual images? We nevertheless have the joy and privilege of the doing, the learning, the growing, the utilizing of what has been given us, and each time we do, the doing of it is intensely personal, meaningful, worth doing and doing well. Even though others may have accomplished something similar before, it is new to each of us. Only through applying knowledge can wisdom be gained and understanding realized.

In Proverbs 13:19a, it is written: "The desire accomplished is sweet to the soul." And it is, as all of you who have accomplished something, anything, well know. Therefore, do not be dismayed, even for a moment, that creativity is not available. Let the world have its creativity, its plagiarism, its envy, strife and pride. What edification does it lend but self-aggrandizement to people (which is a trap)? We do not need it.

Let God be the magnificent Creator and let us be the faithful stewards of all He has put into our hands to utilize. He has given more than enough for everyone of us to do, to accomplish and to enjoy in a dozen lifetimes.

Considering God and His Word, we can develop ourselves: steward our abilities and our surroundings; follow His wonderful example; do things; accomplish projects; bring to pass spectacles, shows, music, paintings; have the great joy and even greater joy in sharing with the rest of the Body of Christ.

As it is written in Ecclesiastes 9:10: "Whatsoever thy hand findeth to do, do *it* with thy might; for *there is* no work, nor device, nor knowledge, nor wisdom, in the grave, whither thou goest." And in Colossians 3:23 and 24: "And whatsoever ye do, do *it* heartily, as to the Lord, and not unto men; knowing that of the Lord ye shall receive the reward of the inheritance: for ye serve the Lord Christ.''

OUR FIRST PRIORITY

I have endeavored in this series of essays to build vision of the significance and the necessity of Word-centered culture. Remember, what we look at, we become. We are surrounded by material things in the world and these things can be inspired by the true God and accomplished by believers to the edification of the entire one Body of Christ in love.

For each one of us, no matter how we choose to develop our soul life and to contribute to the one Body, once again I cannot stress enough times that our first priority be the WORD of GOD—growing daily, prevailing daily. We all need to be rooted and grounded, settled and established in God's Word.

There is no way the Word will evidence itself in the works of our minds and hands until it lives and abounds in our individual lives so that the true and living God can be our sole spiritual inspiration and strength. This is for all of us—there can be no exceptions. Each one of us walks first before Him.

To grow quickly, solidly in that Word, I can think of no better programs than those this ministry makes available—The Way Corps, the WOW Ambassadors, Advanced Studies, and Foundational Classes, again and again and again. It may take a few years to get God's Word really settled into one's heart. However, if the lord tarries, WOW is a year's commitment; The Way Corps—four years. Not everyone has it in his heart to be a Limb coordinator or a Branch coordinator. Then what else do you want to do with your life?

Once the Word is rooted and grounded, all the doors to developing our soul lives are opened in any direction. God will take us as far as we care to go with Him.

For you who are reading this, if you are young and do not yet know where your interests or abilities lie, try *something*, do *something* and tackle it with all of God's ability in Christ in you. You are bound to learn *something* about God, about yourself and about other people. Learning is never a loss.

If you are already developing a particular ability—in art school, in college, in drama school, in music school, engineering, medical school, etc., let God's Word so live in your mind that you can separate the truth of what you are being taught from the error. And go ahead—you are free to excel. What better witness to those around you than to learn quickly or to do brilliantly in some field? Ask God to help you and to teach you. He is faithful; He is at hand.

And then, if the lord tarries, in time you can be that expert cameraman to film the Rock of Ages 1994. You can be that expert writer of the books God's people are waiting for that will entertain, inform and build believing in the true God. You, too, can be that excellent actor for the plays we will produce for God's people. You, too, can compose that brilliant music for the occasion of a future anniversary of The Way International, in which the Word vibrates magnificently in every musical phrase building vision in each heart of God's greatness, grandeur and majesty. You may sing that solo with breathtaking ease and mastery that puts in the mind of the audience: Yes, this is the human voice that God gave, richly developed.

It is available. It is all available. You, too, can design dwellings and build them with love so that every window frame, every hinge, reflects God's care, God's thoughtfulness, God's attention to detail. You too can grow the food which is blessed by God and your hands to meet the physical needs of the saints. You too can run your business to the praise and glory to God.

What a Body of which to be a part! What a life God has set before each one of us! What a time to be alive! Let us cast aside all vestiges of leftover fears and let us rise to meet the adventure in living to which God has invited us. Let us begin. Let us decide to excel, to glorify Him by the superior excellence which He Himself has called us to, whatever our field of endeavor. The field of endeavor does not matter. What do you want to do? For with God nothing shall be impossible.

Part Two

It Is Written:
Essays in Culture

The State of the Union

THE STATE OF THE UNION

If I were president of this land,
This is how I'd make my stand:

I'd expose the national mess
In my opening address.

But having laid bare the despair,
I would hurry on from there.

Pausing, I'd show how to look
For the answers in God's Book.

Classes I would plan on giving
In Power for Abundant Living—

For the Bible speaks solutions
To all problems and pollutions,

And the Bible states the answer
For the soldier and the dancer.

Alas, or Yea!

Chief of state's not in my scheme;
My calling: Pen and paper and a dream.

    Personally, I liked the observations of Tony Manero,

hero of "Saturday Night Fever," on the state of the Union. At a point of sudden insight, with his forlorn face magnified on the screen, he declares: "Everybody's dumping. The whole world is dumping. (Pause—flashbulb in brain.) Even humping is dumping." To translate Tony's insight into more universal terms: the whole world is taking a crap, disposing of its waste, giving its worst. That is the quality of giving in the world today. Even "humping" (sexual intercourse) is no more than an unloading of one's worst. Sexual intercourse, the act through which the highest degree of marital love, intimacy, giving and fellowship might be communicated, is today totally corrupted into its reverse—the flushing away of one's wastes.

I liked Tony's observations because they summed up the truth so clearly and succinctly: Our culture today is a consumer society, and consequently, as the quality of Tony's phraseology might indicate, an illiterate society. Both of these terms need explanation.

Consumer society, or a nation of consumers,—the "gimme-kid" society—puts its emphasis exactly on that. "What can I get?" Something for nothing is its underlying premise. This emphasis however is the exact reverse of what the Word of God teaches. In light of the Word, "What can I get?" is an inaccurate, indeed an impossible, question. The only valid question one might ask is "What can I give?" Now, that is a real, true and accurate question; and in giving something, one receives. Conversely, it is impossible to receive anything without giving something. Something for nothing is an out-and-out lie, an impossibility.

Zig Ziglar summed up in a single line the basic truth

of all wisdom: "There ain't no free lunches." The only way to receive, to get anything, is to give—to put forth energy (physical, mental or spiritual, or a combination thereof). Giving will result in receiving. But to reverse the emphasis is to perpetrate a lie. And so, the consumer society is a reversal of this truth. In teaching people to seek first what they can get, the society is living and perpetuating a lie as if it were foundational truth.

One of the gravest results of a people living and believing such a lie is *illiteracy*. By using the word "illiteracy," I am pushing the word to include its deeper meaning. "Literacy" is, broadly, the ability to read. "Illiteracy" is the opposite, the inability to read. By reading, I am insisting on the deeper Biblical meaning of the word (to be more thoroughly discussed in the essay entitled "On Reading"). It is not merely an ability to pronounce a word, but includes understanding the meaning of the word in its scope and context, or being able to interpret that word with impact on the mind. Reading, Biblically, includes two phases: (1) reading the writing, and (2) shewing the interpretation thereof.

It is one thing to "read the writing," but that is not all there is to reading. Now, the writing must be read—there can be no interpretation unless the writing is read—but to read the writing alone is not literacy as I am using the word here.

Our statistical figures on literacy in this country are fairly high. I have little doubt that many people can look at and read the writing on signs, newspapers and books; but I do not believe they are interpreting the meanings of these words to any high degree. Our language has become meaningless to large segments of the public. Witness the craze of the fifties and sixties for the monosyllabic, four-letter-word vocabulary, in which the word "cool" meant "good" as well as its exact opposite, "bad." Later still, in some areas of the culture, "bad" came to mean "good," confusing the language even more. Observe also our politicians, the nation's leaders, who say one thing and mean another.

The use of words—language—has become meaningless on a large scale. One need not search far to find that words have lost meaning in people's minds and mouths and that a lack of *meaningful* vocabulary leads to a breakdown of fellowship or meaningful communications between people—no meaningful words, no communication, no fellowship and no thinking. Thinking requires meaningful words. Not thinking opens the undisciplined mind to any kind of influence. Not thinking results in extreme frustration and violence, in disorder and the loss of freedom, in possession by outside negative forces, and in destruction. Man was made to think, to say and to do. Illiteracy, the lack of meaningful words, gravely hinders him from accomplishing these functions.

Allow me to tack down the general comments above to something more specific. "Saturday Night Fever" is a highly accurate picture of the consumer-illiterate society which is the state of the Union today. To make my meaning clear, I should like to discuss this film in further detail.

"Saturday Night Fever" revolves around a nineteen-year-old hero, Tony Manero, who, in his native

Brooklyn, works in a drab, uninspiring paint store selling paint. He lives with his family: his construction-worker father, many months unemployed; his grandmother, a first-generation immigrant who speaks little English; his mother, whose whole reason for living rests on her older son, a Catholic priest, who in her eyes is successful and gives her her only sense of value; and finally, a younger sister, as yet fairly bright and uncontaminated by the generally dull and heavily negative surroundings.

Tony's life consists of work, hanging out with his buddies, and the high point, dressing up and going to the local disco on Saturday nights. There, he is the bright star, for he has taught himself to dance. There, he glows amid the adulation of his peers, the sighs of admiring girls who offer themselves to him sexually from every side. There, he receives recognition, the praise of men, admiration, validation. There, once a week on Saturday night he is somebody—a person who has something to give.

Tony is attracted to a young lady, also a dancer, and this attraction starts him on his way to the possibility of changing his life for something better. In any case, at the end of the film we are left with the hope that he may come up and out.

The film opens with helicopter shots of the Brooklyn Bridge—the symbol for "a bridge to something better." We see Tony at work, Tony at home and Tony with his buddies. In the opening scenes he runs along with the world around him. But gradually the main ingredient of the hero emerges—a certain quality of meekness, a desire to change, a quest for something better. As this quality manifests itself, he begins to differ more and more strikingly from the people around him and becomes more like the girl who has already made the move from Brooklyn to Manhattan—changed, having found something better through knowledge.

What was so accurate about this film as I saw it? In America today, over seventy-five percent of the population lives in cities of over 100,000—in other words, large cities. More than seventy-five percent of the population lives urban-style, surrounded by the works of men's hands, separated from God's creation. In such an environment, the disco dance floor has usurped the places of fellowship available in previous eras.

For example, let us compare Greece in the Golden Age (fifth century B.C.) to our society today. In this bygone era, schools of rhetoric and oratory were prominent. There young men learned to speak and master the usage of words to persuade men. The place of fellowship, of commerce and communication, was the marketplace. The marketplace was the center of public life, where men spoke words, reasoning and persuading; there they shone and received admiration and recognition from their fellowmen.

On the physical side, there were the games—all throughout ancient Greece and later in the Roman Empire the games were a way of life. Young men (and women) were trained from an early age to participate in these athletic games in which their physical prowess, speed, coordination and beauty were publicly recognized, admired and praised. So there were two major avenues in which men could excel, prove themselves, set examples, "be somebody" in ancient society.

But we need not go so far back in history. In the infancy of our own country, the fathers of our Constitution—John Adams, Thomas Jefferson and others—had a so-called "classical education" which included the study of Greek and Latin, not for speaking, but to build mental discipline and constructive mental processes.

Who did they read in Greek and Latin? Why, of course, the great orators of ancient Greece and Rome. What kind of exercises did they write in Latin and Greek? Great orations, rhetoric, of course. Thus, they practiced the usage and control of words, and primarily in foreign, even extinct, languages. What mental discipline such study built is evidenced in the speeches and writings of these men. They communicated with one another. They shared fellowship.

The physical arena during the same era in our land was embodied in the quest to subdue the wilderness. These early Americans lived upon a wild, virgin land which provided ground for physical victories that could be praised and admired by other men.

Today, where are our schools of rhetoric, or oratory? Who learns to read, to speak, to persuade with words? What forums are there for recognition in these areas? And physically, where can a man excel for all the world to see? Yes, there are football games, baseball games; but the public presentation of these is nearly limited to a few professional teams.

What is there for the Tony Manero of today, the big-city punk who never learned to speak because his parents, in their turn, did not learn either? Today, the marketplace and the arena both have been buried under our mega-cities, and on their ruins sits the two-bit local disco dance floor.

What more appropriate meeting place for the illiterate society than the disco dance floor, with music forceful and loud, drowning out any possibility for the exchange of meaningful words? In the illiterate society, where most can neither express themselves nor communicate their thoughts or feelings, the disco dance floor at least provides a central point for people to come physically together.

Where the skilled use of words has become extinct as an avenue of giving and receiving, there remains the physical only. And where there are no games to master, our boy learns to dance. Here on the dance floor, in the darkened heart of megalopolis, Tony can show off his skill, his physical training, his self-discipline—he can give something and receive the admiration and praise of others.

At home, in several scenes around the family dinner table, the inability to communicate is so acute that after a few meaningless exchanges, Tony's whole family disintegrates into hitting one another. Failure of understanding, lack of communication (both of which require appropriate and meaningul use of words) cause extreme frustration and thence, violence, hurt and condemnation.

"Saturday Night Fever" contains many more minute details which I would term highly accurate in presenting a picture of American culture today. I dwell on it here not to condemn the film, but to expose its accuracy.

We can more easily change a condition after we have recognized and defined it. And that is what I have been presenting here in broad strokes: the sad state of the Union today. First, I have diagnosed the condition as consumerism (built shakily on a major lie); and second, I have called it illiterate—a state in which words have little meaning, leading to impoverished and futile communication between people and a lack of fellowship.

Loneliness, isolation (even among the materially comfortable), deep frustration, disorder, violence and unnatural death permeate our society.

What is the problem? And, more important, what is the answer? Let me quickly assure you, there is an answer—one close at hand and sure. It is on this answer that the rest of these essays will elaborate with direct reference to you, the individual.

The problems in America today that I have termed consumerism and illiteracy have a spiritual root and a spiritual reason. There is an adversary abroad who is blinding the minds of people so that they cannot come unto a knowledge of the accuracy of God's Word. What greater way to attack than to cause greater and greater illiteracy so that people do not understand words even when they hear them? And if they cannot understand the words of truth, they continue believing the lie: "What can I get?" And they continue living accordingly, earning nothing but death.

The adversary creeps abroad, working hard and stealing fast wherever he can. He has been working for millenniums. His most successful tools in the last generation have been TV, drugs and dropping out as a life-style.

In other eras, other generations, he has used other approaches. But these are his methods today to cover our educated society with a broad blanket of illiteracy that tears down fellowship, believing and like-mindedness.

What greater incentive could we have than to know the truth and to combat his influence spiritually? The answer is the Word of God. To properly utilize and apply the answer, a person must come to the Word and be able to read or hear and understand words; that is to be literate in the sense that I have described it.

Man is basically God-hungry. He hungers for the richness of fellowship with God. Only then can he have meaningful fellowship (communication, relationships, giving and receiving) with other people also.

To have the seed of spiritual fellowship with God, one must simply carry out Romans 10:9 and 10:

> That if thou shalt confess with thy mouth the Lord Jesus, and shalt believe in thine heart that God hath raised him from the dead, thou shalt be saved.
> For with the heart man believeth unto righteousness; and with the mouth confession is made unto salvation.

Once believed, these words usher in the new birth. A person is born again. He has eternal life. This seed cannot be extinguished. But from this point, the quality of his life, his fellowship with God, can be only as great as his knowledge and application of the Word of God in his life.

The battleground is in the mind. The job of renewing one's mind is a continuous and daily process until our lord's return, which could be today or tomorrow or a hundred years from now. Since we do not know the times or the seasons of his return, it behooves us to get cracking on our major "good work," our main job—renewing our minds to the greatness and accuracy of the Word of God. It is for the purpose of setting in mind some helpful tools to accomplish this job that I am writing the essays which follow.

Our minds are the theaters of war in this continuous spiritual battle. Our minds are reached through our five senses and through the spirit of God which lives in us. However, even if the spirit of God lives in us, we can utilize the power of Christ in us only to the degree that we understand the Word of God in our minds.

The adversary's major attack today is always upon God's Word, endeavoring to keep it from reaching people lest they be born again, and then, with a knowledge of God's power in their minds, win the upper hand over him. I have tagged his major tools today as TV, drugs and dropping out. He is using these tools to blind people, lowering a cloud of illiteracy over the land.

The weapon of God is His Word *in the mind*. His Word enters a person's mind through hearing or reading AND UNDERSTANDING THE WORDS. The ability to read effectively and understand what one reads is in direct proportion to that person's life and living—to his experience of life.

Words on a page are abstract symbols. If I had grown up in the deserts of central Australia where there are no trees and I had never seen a tree, when I saw the word "tree" written, it would have no meaning to me. Now, I could ask someone or look it up in a book—the meaning of "tree." I could get a description, even a drawing or sketch. And henceforth, whenever I saw the word "tree," I would have a frame of reference, but not a very broad one.

On the other hand, suppose I had grown up in New England on a farm and from an early age had watched trees bloom, die and bloom again—had sat under their shade on heat-soaked days, had smelled their blossoms, picked and investigated their leaves, had leaned against the roughness of their bark, scraped my shoulder while climbing their limbs, chewed the stems of twigs. In other words, suppose I had been intimately involved with trees all my life. Coming across the word "tree" written on a page, that black-and-white symbol would evoke sights, smells, tastes, feelings, textures, colors— experiences of great depth. That word "tree" would have a mind-filling meaning for me. This is what I mean by one's ability to read being in direct proportion to one's experience of life.

The TV, drugs and dropping out—today's thieves— suck people like a vacuum cleaner right out of life and living. From early childhood they draw the individual away from exposure to experience that would lay a groundwork for effective reading later. There are exceptions, of course. These thieves have only as much influence over people as the people allow them to have. But the Tony Maneros in today's megalopolis become subject to these influences because, in contrast, their surroundings are so overwhelmingly drab, so dull, so secondhand, that TV, drugs and dropping out seem the lesser of two evils. Evils, nevertheless, are both alternatives.

Reading the Word of God is the major avenue to

receiving a knowledge of God. That is why I begin with reading. We can listen to tapes and attend live teachings of the Word, but our continued fellowship with God depends on the solidity of our individual relationship with His written Word. Our relationship with God depends on where we stand in relation to "IT IS WRITTEN."

When I lived in Manhattan, I was acquainted with a family whose world ended at 14th Street. they could hardly imagine a sphere existing outside of a five-block radius. Their small child's babysitter every waking hour was the TV. Their older son, in junior high school, was already a step-sitting glue-sniffer and was well on his way to dropping out of school and, thence, out of life. They were tightly wrapped in the clutches of today's thieves. They were not the only family in New York which lived that way.

TV, drugs and dropping out, the prevailing life-styles of many in our big cities, are darkening people's minds with a dense blindness. When one is dominated by these elements year after year, what does a person have left to give? If he has nothing left to give, what can he then receive?

So the thieves steal life and living from people. Without life and living, without exposure to experience, people have no reason to develop and use meaningful words. Without meaningful words, people cannot fellowship together—meaningful giving and receiving. What is there to live for? communication has broken down. As Tony lamented, "Everyone is dumping. Even humping is dumping."

In other eras, other cultures, other societies (before

TV), the campfire or fireside provided a gathering place for people. In the days of Homer (Troy, 800 B.C.), it was around the campfire that people gathered after days of heavy work. And by its warm, flickering light the bard would recite the epic battles of the gods to an enthralled audience.

In the days of King Arthur or the medieval kings, in a castle or a lowly hut, at evening the fellowship around a blazing log would resound with song, or hush at the thrill of poetry, or glow with the merriment of a joke. Around the fireside, fellowship thrived—giving and receiving.

In the days of our own country's westward expansion, after daylong travel in Conestoga wagons beneath heat-blasting sun, the wagon train formed into a circle in the cool of the evening. In its center, seated around a campfire, all the weary travelers gathered. Here again, fellowship was shared. Perhaps there were reminiscences of the life left behind; perhaps they revealed their aspirations for the life ahead—a genuine exhange transpired between individuals, providing comfort, satisfaction and rest for all who were present.

In these last decades; it is as though the adversary has smitten that very campfire, beating it with the blunt poker of his methods and scattering it across the land. Sparks have flown—small, cold sparks—today, each one being the TV set in a private home where one or more silent humans sit, eyes glazed, before its jumping, lifeless images, seeking in this cold spark the warmth of that long-gone fellowship which was once so richly shared around the crackling campfire.

Let me draw some further implications from this

illustration. Throughout the Word of God, fire is associated with the presence of God—with fellowship with God. From Moses and the children of Israel, who moved through the wilderness behind a pillar of fire by night, to the day of Pentecost when "...there appeared unto them cloven tongues like as of fire, and it sat upon each of them. And they were all filled with the Holy Ghost..." (Acts 2:3 and 4), fire is associated in the Word of God with the visible workings of the Holy Spirit; and through cumulative usage, we can look at it as a symbol of fellowship with God.

Likewise, the campfire of eras gone by were centers of fellowship with God. For only as men have fellowship with Him can they have real fellowship with one another.

I John 1:3:
That which we have seen and heard declare we unto you, that ye also may have fellowship with us: and truly our fellowship *is* with the Father, and with his Son Jesus Christ.

Those who basked in the warmth of the campfire experienced that atmosphere so necessary for the giving and receiving of the best qualities of their lives.

Today, where are those campfires? Is it not far more common to find lonely and aimless individuals in many, many isolated living rooms, trying to warm themselves before that glassed-in spark of the videoscreen, a faint counterfeit of the campfire that once really drew people together?

How many children, having grown up in our mechanized cities and having been babysat by the TV set, have drawn the conclusion that milk comes from milk cartons, that vegetables "appear" in the super-market?

How many uncounted minds, severed from the works of God's hands, have been isolated from the real learning so easily available in nature, God's creation?

TV, drugs and dropping out—the major thieves of the consumer life-style today—steal from us the experience of life and the reason to develop meaningful words.

Recently I found myself in company with a group of people in their twenties. One of them had never heard of the Crusades. Another disclosed, in the course of our conversation, he had no idea when or where the First World War had been fought, or the Second either, for that matter. Further conversation revealed early involvement in drugs, subsequent suspension and dropping out of school followed by several years of purposeless wandering, having dropped out of society.

Up through the 1940s, and even into the fifties, the general national requirement to stay in high school through graduation insured a certain basic level of "general education." But not so in these days.

What I am stressing here is the importance of reading and understanding words in relation to life and living. The practical answers to everday life in all aspects are contained in the Word of God. And after one has been born again, engrafting God's Word into one's mind is basically accomplished through *reading*.

Understanding what is read has a direct relationship to the fullness of one's experiences in life. Through TV, drugs and dropping out, the younger generation is early deprived of life and living. When that person finally comes to the Word of God, he has little mental discipline and no solid mental structures upon which to pattern relationships with the Word.

Compensation for this lack of real living experience is one of the important functions of The Way Corps program. In The Way Corps, the Tony Maneros once again have to do basic work, get their hands dirty, sweat, apply themselves—in direct contradiction to the philosophy of the totally undisciplined "gimme-kid" society from which they often come. Many of us who entered The Way Corps came in with sloppy mud puddles for minds. In the Corps, we were pulled away from the influence of these three major thieves and given a chance to develop some basic mental discipline.

Along with the demand to give and put forth energy (by getting up early, running, working, keeping a certain schedule), the Corps provides daily doses of the Word of God. Because the Word of God is "quick, and powerful, and sharper than any twoedged sword," this combination can hardly fail to build a solid mental structure in the mind of anyone desiring to see wholeness in his own life.

I have painted a picture of the adversary's devices in our times to whet your desire (and mine) to stand and withstand in this day and time. At times a jolt of righteous anger is what it takes to make me determined to cut through the garbage and walk ahead for God.

Yes, the adversary is at work. Yes, he is subtle; he is busy. Yes, the battleground is in the individual mind. BUT GOD has provided an absolutely foolproof way to combat the adversary's influences upon our daily lives. God has enabled us to come to a knowledge of

His Word through The Way Ministry. God has made a deeper knowledge of His Word available to more believers today than at any time in history. This is almost unbelieveably awe-inspiring to me, that God's Word should be so richly available today, of all days; and that by some unfathomable quirk, or rather by the infinite grace of God, we are here to partake of it.

Now since God has planted irrevocably that seed of eternal life within us, my constant and searching question is: How do we instill His Word, in all its fullness, scope, application and awareness, into our minds?

It is to share some insights into this question that I have set down the following essays. Broadly, their subject matter is the application of the renewed mind.

The renewed mind involves thinking. How does the mind work? How do I gain total control (yes, total control is available) over it? How do I transform my mind from a sloppy mud puddle, in which a herd of inarticulate feelings once wallowed, into a structure that can think and understand the Word?

I have found my mind to be a fascinating toy, a machine, a computer—highly demanding, always in motion—and I have had to work with it unceasingly. When I have let it go, it has caused me unbearable suffering; but by the same token, when controlled, guided, directed, it has brought me the greatest, inexplicable pleasures and joys—those that come only from being in total fellowship with God, my heavenly Father. There is no higher plane we may occupy; yet it is not a stationary plane either, for we can grow constantly in our awareness, appreciation, enjoyment and depth of this fellowship with Him. He always has more to give us.

We can never outgrow God. So, do not hesitate to grow in your renewed mind as rapidly and as broadly as you are able. Do not hesitate to expand the scope and quality of your fellowship with Him.

Now that we have seen some dimensions of the problem, let us look to the solution. Our real concern is with the how of building God's Word into one's mind. The essays that follow are on separate aspects of this theme. They will be most readily received by those who are already born again and who have already begun endeavoring to deal with their own minds minute by minute, day after day, in the light of God's Word.

If I were addressing my words to new babes in Christ, I would emphasize and reemphasize, state and restate, the basic foundational truths of the indwelling Christ and the operation of the manifestations of the spirit.

I would exhort people again and again to hear the foundational class on Power for Abundant Living, to work it into their lives, to memorize the foundational verses.

This is what others did for me, and I cannot thank them enough. But there came a time when I began to believe at some basic level of understanding the foundational truths taught in that class. Then I began to place more emphasis, not on my own receiving, but on bringing that gift from God, the whole package of inherent dynamite, into detailed manifestation.

This quest began to consume much of the energy of my thoughts. How could I bring out that gift in a continuous, non-sporadic flow, so I could see it, in my soul, in my body and in my surroundings constantly?

These essays are the result of principles from the Word of God that I have worked in my own life. I am setting forth avenues of action which helped me to work the Word of God into my own mind. They are by no means the only avenues available. My prayer and believing is that some of these lines of thought may be an inspiration to you, something workable, that will energize or revitalize the Word in your mind.

Truly, in all our parts, including our minds, we are "fearfully *and* wonderfully made," as the Psalmist has said. I have read the works of several psychologists that claim that most people utilize in their lifetimes only ten to fifteen percent of their mental capacities. How psychologists measure the percentage of mental use I cannot fathom, so I do not comprehend the grounds for this claim. Yet, the figure seems logical to me.

God formed, made and created Adam, a wonderful, perfect man. God in His foreknowledge knew that Christ would come centuries later, and that after his death and resurrection would come the day of Pentecost and the Administration of Grace in which you and I live. God knew that "Christ in you" would be available one day.

God also knew that once we were born again, we could bring into evidence only as much of the "Christ in us" as resided in our renewed minds. If, after we were born again, the "Christ in us" could operate *without* our minds, outside the freedom of our wills, that would be possession. However, this is not the case. God in Christ in us operates through our renewed mind believing. He never tampers with the freedom of our will, but makes everything available by believing.

We can believe only what we know.

So God made Adam, and He made his mind one that could receive, retain and release the greatness of His spirit within. Is it surprising, since Christ within was not available until about 2,000 years ago, that men used only a small part of that total mental capacity? And still do?

It is our working of God's Word, and His working in us through Christ, that expands and refines the working capacity of our minds. The more Christ I comprehend in myself, with my mind, the more I can evidence. The "Christ in me" which I fail to hold in my mind, I fail to manifest.

We all have the same measure of power through Christ within. Each one of us is able to operate the same power that God utilized in raising him from among the dead after three days. The difference among believers is the depth of the mental comprehension of Christ within that they hold.

So let the psychologists say the average man uses ten percent of his brain power in a lifetime. That inspires my resolve—there is ninety percent more to develop. How exciting! God gave us minds that could comprehend the Christ within.

Truly the renewed mind is the key to power. Perhaps even in the act of setting down these themes I shall learn more and be forced to think more clearly, with further vision through the light of God's Word. These essays are explorations, adventures in thinking in the light of God's Word. Let them bless your life and add inspiration and understanding to your walk and fellowship with Him.

I began this series of essays by characterizing our society today as a consumer society and as an illiterate society. Illiteracy I have defined as not grasping what is read. What better way for the adversary to keep people from the Word of God than by perpetuating and increasing a general illiteracy?

Therefore in my first essay, I handle *reading* from the Word of God. To put the Word in our minds, sooner or later, after all the tapes and live teachings, after all the vocal sharings, we must read the Word. So I handle some aspects of what is involved in reading and how to read. For reading, real reading, is a highly developed state of mental discipline.

Because we understand reading better in relation to its counterpart, I next handle writing. Like freedom and responsibility, or giving and receiving, reading and writing are two sides of the same process. Again, writing is presented in the light of the Word of God.

My goal in each essay is to energize the Christ within by controlling the mind. The renewed mind involves thinking—asking "what?" and "how?" The next essay concentrates on some lines of thinking through forms, and is especially addressed to the artists of our ministry.

These essays are loosely connected. All fall under the general theme of how to work God's Word into one's mind. In the fifth and final essay of this collection, several conclusions are drawn.

Why is this collection called *It Is Written: Essays in Culture*? Because once the Christ within is dwelling richly in our minds, Christ cannot help but evidence himself in our lives. When we think the Word of God, really think it with understanding, we will consequently speak it and do it. Once grasped in our minds, Christ within CANNOT BE HID but will be in evidence in detail in the senses realm. And that means we will have a Word-centered culture—if the lord tarries.

Ah, it is out! My ulterior motive is bared! I seek a life-style imbued with things made and services performed from the wellspring of the love of God in others. I myself need to produce works and serve in the Body of Christ from the wellspring of the love of God planted in me. If the lord tarries, I desire to see the building and blossoming of the one Body evidenced in a Word-centered culture. How about you?

In these essays, I am concentrating on that possible bottleneck—that point of actually getting God's Word into the mind. "Thoughts are the seeds for our words and our deeds." I have found that if I concentrate on this point, engaging my mind with the Word, the words and actions are then the fruit. But how to work the Word into my mind has at times baffled, confused or eluded me.

This is the point to which the following thoughts are consciously addressed. God bless you richly, dear reader. Enjoy the fellowship as you read. By God's grace and mercy, seeds of riches shall be planted in your mind, also, to come simply into fruition in time of harvest.

Essay Two

On Reading

Y ou must be a reader, since your eyes are scanning this page. I have caught you in the very act! Have you ever stopped to consider what it is you are doing? And exactly how you are doing it? I believe that our continued, vital relationship with God depends on the solidity of our individual, personal and intimate relationship with God's WRITTEN WORD. More than anyone, the believers of our ministry stake their lives on the truth and accuracy of God's written Word: IT IS WRITTEN!

Teachings are inspiring—live or on tape. That fellowship with other believers, even a short exchange about the weather, can comfort, exhort, reprove, correct and bless. But notice, I said *continued* fellowship with God. Lively, spoken words may inspire us into godliness at the time, but the times come when there are no tapes available, when we are on our own somewhere, perhaps surrounded by unbelievers. The times must come when it is finally you and your relationship with God's written Word, the Bible. And at this point reading is essential.

It has helped me to set reading in its proper and broader context. Reading is inescapably bound with *writing*. For what we read is writing, something written. And what is written is a bunch of letters or marks strung together, forming *words*. *Reading, writing, words*—this is the broader context of reading. What was written were words. The *words* were *written* to be read by somebody at sometime.

What are written words? Look at a page of writing. This page will do as well as any. Pages of writing are monotonously similar at a glance—rows and rows of bunches of little black marks. They are not even pretty. They do not move, do not dance. They do not project much aroma (except occasionally that of fresh ink). They do not sing sweetly, or croon in your ear. Touch the page. Unless embossed (or in Braille), the marks cannot be felt with the fingertips. And they do not reach out and touch you.

Oh, what a nothing! What a foolishness! What are these stupid little black things good for? What is their fascination? What is their power?

Now, here is the crux. Words are power. Among all that man produces, words have the greatest influence over our minds and over the minds of other people. Dumb as they seem, lined up here obediently in rows on the page like companies of soldiers in formation, words do have the greatest power over people, greater power than bombs or armies.

Man's body is controlled by his mind. A man's mind is controlled by ideas—the beliefs that it holds. Ideas can commence as feelings, impulses, pictures, graphs or charts; but put into words, ideas are communicable in the greatest detail, the most refined specifics, the most precise clarity. Of all the media available to man to communicate ideas, words are potentially the most economical, the most efficient, the most specific, precise, accurate and therefore the most powerful.

My total conviction in this matter is founded on the fact that God chose words—written words which He magnified above all His name (Psalms 138:2b)—to make Himself known unto man. He could have told man to erect buildings, paint pictures, draw charts or graphs, write symphonies, build cities, etc., as a primary way to make Himself known. But although God has inspired man to produce many works, God chose words through which to declare Himself conclusively and vitally to mankind. I am sure God knew what He was (and is) doing.

Communication is anything that moves people who move ideas that move people. So, at the height of the Roman Empire (when 51,000 miles of paved roads connected much of Europe, Africa and the Middle East), roads were the major avenue of communication. Along the Roman roads, people with ideas moved into the presence of other people, who received the ideas and moved other people.

Today, the television set and the radio bring people with ideas into our very living rooms, and these ideas move us to act. Roads, ships, cars, TV, radio, books, newspapers, telephone, telegraph—all these media move people with ideas that move other people to move the ideas to move others, etc. When someone *moves* on an idea, communication has definitely taken place.

The vehicles of communication enumerated above can move people with ideas, BUT, the people with the ideas must utilize words to get their ideas across to others.

There are basically only two kinds of words—spoken and written. What a spoken and a written word have in common are WORDS. A spoken word is heard. A written word is read. Words are the common media of both these forms of communication. However, there is a vast difference in the use and application of words in these two media which it is helpful to consider, since we are all *users* of words, both written and spoken.

Words can exert the greatest control over the mind. Words are symbols of things and ideas. Ideas control men. They influence people to act.

Consider now the differences between a spoken word and a written word. A spoken word is immediate. A spoken word is alive and present. A spoken word has the believing and conviction of the speaker behind it. The speaker, if seasoned in understanding, has much to work with. He has his body. He can keep the attention of a listener by moving his body, by using his eyes, by cutting the air with a vivid gesture. The speaker has his actual, living presence to keep the senses of his listeners tuned into his message. He can modulate his voice, shout a phrase, then drop his voice to a whisper, causing his audience to strain forward to hear. When he notes a blankness of expression, the speaker can tailor his illustration, restate his message in a different way, put forward an additional example. The speaker has his whole dynamic body and presence, his believing and conviction, to work with to insure that his listeners receive his message.

A spoken word (on the lips of an experienced and masterful speaker) has a vividness, a reality, an immediacy that potentially fills the mind of his listener with his words (ideas). The listener forgets his laundry, his tired feet, his grudge against his neighbor. He allows his mind, through his eyes and ears, to be filled with the words of the speaker. And this is the speaker's aim. For the speaker speaks because he is convinced that his ideas are worthy of being heard, grasped and digested by his listener.

Now, a certain amount of willingness or receptivity on the part of the listener is necessary also. But, if the speaker is forceful, knows his medium and uses all that is available to him, his spoken words will have the power to fill the mind of his listener, to overwhelm all his extraneous thoughts and make the listener's mind a reproduction of his own mind for that time. He can thus, through words, transfer his ideas in detail into the listener's mind. Thus a spoken word has tremendous life and power. Spoken words will sometimes ring in the listener's ears with the force and presence of the speaker for hours, even days.

But here is the inherent limitation of the spoken word. Alive and vibrant when spoken, it fades eventually, evaporating from the mind. The listener walks out from the presence of the speaker, and his five senses are immediately bombarded by his surroundings—the smell of the grass, the presence of other people, a pressing concern. He is suddenly hungry. The realities of his life, the sights, smells, tastes, sounds and feelings of the world around him wash over his mind like the rising tide. The spoken words he has just heard are carried away, becoming harder and harder to recall from the sea of his senses. A week later, he cannot speak verbatim those spoken words he heard. He may produce a weak and watered-down paraphrase.

Have you ever played the child's game, "Telephone"? Perhaps you had another name for it. As children we would sit in a circle and one would whisper a phrase or sentence into the ear of his neighbor, who would then pass it on, and so on until it passed all around the circle. Finally, the last player would say aloud the message as he had heard it. If number one had started with something like: "I think you're very pretty," the last player in the circle would come up with something like, "I hope you're not too dirty." The game always gave us some good laughs on a rainy afternoon. It helps to illustrate for us the truth that a spoken word, besides fading quickly from the mind, is inclined also to change quickly, to end up a few people down the line saying not at all what it started out to say.

We are all merchants, trading in the spoken word every day—whether we exchange one-on-one in quiet company, share at a Twig with a dozen or teach the Word of God to thousands. We are all users who can be masters, if we consider its potential and utilize to the hilt what is available to us in a spoken word. We aim for people to understand our message, as we understand it, for them to follow it, and finally, to act upon it. And indeed, when someone moves on the idea that we have spoken, it is a sure sign that it was understood. Our words are important and powerful and deserve our most careful thought.

As it is written in Matthew 12:36 and 37:

But I say unto you, That every idle word that men shall

speak, they shall give account thereof in the day of judgment.

For by thy words thou shalt be justified, and by thy words thou shalt be condemned.

So much for a brief excursion into the nature of the spoken word with its dynamic power in the immediate moment and its built-in limitations, fading as quickly as it is spoken and inclined to change with the hearing.

The nature of a written word is another matter. Remember, as with a spoken word, the medium is WORDS. However, in their written form they are now stacked in rows on page after unappealing page, words, words, words—little, motionless black marks in self-satisfied groupings on a white background.

What shall we say then to these things? The speaker is not present. His voice, face, body, the power of his presence are all absent. You, the reader, are alone, staring at the page. You must read the writing.

But there is even more to reading. From the point of view of the writer, the words must be chosen with even greater thought, clarity of vision and judgment than are spoken words. (There is, of course, volume upon volume of lousy writing from which the most adept reader will receive nothing but annoyance, since the writer wrote nothing worth putting into one's mind.) The writer I am postulating is a great one—a clear thinker, a master of words—as were, for example, the writers of God's Word.

There are two reasons for this care in choosing written words. First of all, the writer is not present to defend, explain or give another illustration. He cannot shout and whisper to keep attenion, cannot glare meaningfully with his eyes, cannot wave his hand or jump up and down. The speaker, the writer, is not here. His words must speak for themselves. The written word must stand for itself (we shall explore this whole area in further detail in the following essay, "On Writing"). The writer, therefore, must exercise the most acute judgment in his selection of words.

He must take care for a second reason also: a written word is not inclined to change. A written word stays the same, through centuries, through space. A written word stands. We can refer to it again and again, and, unless it has been altered by someone, that word always says the same thing. Therefore, unlike spoken words which tend to change in memory, a written word looked at weeks or years later will say exactly the same thing it said when first written. Furthermore, a written word, simply because it is written, carries a certain inherent believability. People tend to believe it is true just because it is in print (this fact puts added responsiblity on the writer).

Now, what is reading and what is the reader's responsibility? To read is to make written words come alive in one's mind, in five-senses reality, like a movie running through the mind. When a written word comes alive inside through reading, it can be savored, inhaled, felt, seen, and above all, HEARD.

As that written word comes alive and is heard in the mind, it becomes again a living, spoken word, having the same dynamic immediacy as if the speaker were actually present. The written Word of God is as though God were speaking to you right now.

So the reader's responsibility is to make written

words come alive in his mind. Reading is the mental process which converts a written word once more into a spoken word, putting the reader face-to-face with the speaker. And, because the written word stays the same, the reader may go back again and again. Every time he reads the same passages, the reader enters into the presence of the author himself. If he is reading the Word of God, the reader enters the presence of God, and the vibrant resonance of His very own voice will ring in the reader's ear.

To read for this result, two qualities are necessary: experience of life and stayed-mind concentration. I have been an avid reader from childhood, devouring junk books and great literature in immense quantities throughout the years. However, I readily admit I did not really begin to read—TO READ—until after I had taken the class on Power for Abundant Living, and had begun to apply its principles for awhile, and until I had lived through some real-life situations—joys, disappointments, tragedy—through which words began to have real meaning for me.

At least half of effective reading is the result of how much life one has lived. What did I know at age seventeen about birth, death, raising children, human suffering, about all in a life that can go so wrong or so right? Nevertheless, I read *The Brothers Karamazov*. I read Tolstoi. I read Shakespeare, with his deep understanding of human beings, with his stage strewn with corpses and weeping survivors. And I was bored through huge sections, not because my vocabulary was insufficient, but because I had no depth of life experience to bring to my reading of these men's words.

I am not pushing here for a vast, memorized vocabulary. Studies of schoolchildren today point out that they learn to use many new words from watching television. In fact, breadth of vocabulary has increased significantly among schoolchildren in recent years. However, their minds have only a tenuous hold over these words. Let them watch "Kojak," "Hawaii Five-0" and "Charlie's Angels," and they are blithely using "rape," and "morgue," "corpse," "autopsy," "m.o.," and "investigations" for example. But these words in their mouths are not based on any depth of actual experience. They carry no weight of conviction and exert no life-enriching influence over their minds.

To read effectively, *some* actual experience must be related to the words so that the words can be felt, seen, smelled, tasted, and heard. As I described it in the Introduction, to the degree that I have been involved with real trees, the word "tree" printed on a page will be able to fill the corners of my mind, not with the word "tree," but with the experience of its actuality.

After I was married, had worked, had given birth to children, had lived and experienced a certain amount of life, I brought more understanding, more empathy to my reading. But until I had taken the class on Power for Abundant Living, I did not have in hand the other half of what is needed to read, which is the ability to stay my mind, to concentrate effectively.

Oh, I could do it in short spurts, I suppose. But there was always a cacophony of voices at quiet times (such as when I was reading)—voices concerned with the laundry that needed folding, the dirty windows that needed cleaning, the hunger in my stomach, the disgust with myself over some minute foolishness I had inadvertently committed yesterday, which reminded me of another foolishness (blush)—a terrible foolishness I had instigated last year, which reminded me of when I was eight years old, setting the table, and my sister...and I really need to get up and do something...what's in the refrigerator? Oh, I forgot to shop...shopping list... money...loans...mortgage...if only I could buy....

Such thoughts and images would rush rapaciously in split seconds through my mind, even while my eyes rested on a page of print, from which the words entered my mind weakly, sickly—no match for the competition they had from all the other mental activity. Honestly now, is this example entirely without reference in your own life? Or do you smile knowingly to yourself right now, saying, "Oh, yes, I recognize this pattern. I, too, have been there"?

For me, hearing the Word of God in Power for Abundant Living, being born again of God's Spirit, speaking in tongues—this way of life set so gently before me by the grace of God—began slowly and solidly to bring about a new wholeness in my mind. I began to gain a mental control I had never known before. The multitude of voices gradually faded. Mental flightiness subsided. Longer and longer periods of stayed-mind control over one predominant thought were mine to enjoy, to my immense satisfaction.

Being born again of God brings God's wonderful wholeness and begins to heal our minds so ravaged by years of living according to the course of this world, in the lusts of our flesh, fulfilling the desires of the flesh and of the reprobate, insane mind. Truly, as the scripture says, we were all "by nature the children of wrath, even as others."

God's Word, as it enters our minds, begins to heal us so we are able to concentrate more deeply over longer periods. This discipline is exactly what makes real reading possible.

So the reader needs to bring to reading a certain amount of firsthand experience of life and also a certain amount of stayed-mind discipline, where other thoughts do not distract and mislead the mind from what is being read. Both of these qualities are bound to increase in a growing person—which is anyone who continues in God's Word, no matter what his chronological age or with how much education he begins. Without these two basic ingredients, however, the choicest words of the finest writer, the truths of the greatest author, are like seeds which have no plowed ground to fall upon in the mind of the reader.

The brain cannot distinguish between something vividly imagined and something actually experienced. That is why "imagineering" works. Countless experiments have been done in athletics where, for example, a basketball team was divided into three groups: one practiced so many minutes per day, another group did not practice at all, and the third group did not actually practice, but for so many minutes per day sat down and, as a group, pictured in detail (imagineered) scoring basket after basket.

In experiment after experiment, those who practiced scoring not at all fared the worst in actual performance. But the other two groups (those who actually practiced and those who practiced in the mind) did considerably better, and those who only "imagineered" did even better, in many cases, than those who actually practiced.

This is but one concrete example. To the mind, things vividly imagined are as real as things actually experienced. If this were not true, then renewing the mind to God's Word would be unavailable. But it is. God says we can see things His way no matter what is going on about us.

Reading gives one the opportunity to vividly imagine things not immediately available in one's immediate environment. In fact, any kind of reading helps build one's capacity to imagine vividly. But the reading of the Word of God not only heals and keeps on healing the mind, but also builds constructive patterns of thinking that can be expanded. Reading allows you, the reader, to experience living, to be exposed to people and situations, to experiences and ideas, to problems and solutions not available in your immediate environment. Reading is an excellent building block for the renewed mind, especially the reading of God's words which are pure, not corrupted by error.

Let us go to the Word of God and see what it can show us about reading.

The first use in the Hebrew of the word *qara* (meaning "to call" or "to read") sets a great standard for us:

Exodus 24:7:

And he took the book of the covenant, and read in the audience of the people: and they said, All that the Lord hath said will we do, and be obedient.

Moses read the Word of God to the people. They heard it, and said that they would carry it out. Now, here is a sure sign that people have read a written word—they act on it.

If we continue reading in context, however, we find Moses is then called by God to come up to the holy mount. Moses obeys and stays for forty days, during which time God gives him the Law on two tables of stone, "...written with the finger of God" (Exodus 31:18). The main communication to Moses from God for the subsequent eight chapters contains all the details for the building of the tabernacle.

Now, when Moses returns with the two tables, he finds the people worshiping a golden calf (Exodus 32). In his anger, Moses breaks the tables of the Law. Did not the people say they would obey? Yes, they did. Did they obey? No, here they are already worshiping something other than God. They did not obey what Moses read from the book of the covenant.

As we continue reading, we find that Moses begins *to speak* to the people the things God told him on the mount. In chapter 35, he spells out to them all the details of the tabernacle that God had told him to build. The people then proceed to carry out these instructions according to all that the Lord had spoken to Moses.

Reading is not mentioned again until Deuteronomy. Can we see in Exodus a difference between the use of the spoken word and the written word? The words Moses delivered were to be believed and obeyed. Whether they were spoken or written depended on the need of the moment. Here, the spoken word helped the people carry out what God had said. Yet, to have an unchanging reference point to return to, the written word was essential.

Differences in administrations have an effect here.

Only the man of God, Moses, had the spirit upon him (later, there was Joshua and seventy other leaders); never more than a handful at any one time had a direct line to God. But today, in the Administration of Grace, every born-again believer has Christ in him—a direct, unbreakable line to God through which He can work continually both to will and to do of His good pleasure.

And so Paul, speaking for God to the initiated believer, the faithful in service in the household, in Ephesians 3:4, says:

> Whereby, when ye read, ye may understand my knowledge in the mystery of Christ.

Today when we read, we have the ability to understand spiritually; furthermore, God states emphatically that we may "comprehend with all saints." It is available! Available! God will help us to comprehend not only "the breadth, and length, and depth, and height," but also to know the love of Christ, which passeth understanding, that we may be filled with all the fulness of God!

God desires these things for us. God helps us—as we READ! I am moved. These words resound and reverberate in my mind, shaking the very core of my soul. Do you hear? Do you hear the words? Ah, I wish I could paint them in giant black letters twelve feet high, carve them into the firmament so you would see them in the sky every time you looked up. They are there. These words are Truth.

As we read, we may understand.... As we read, we may understand Paul's knowledge of the Mystery of Christ. This understanding begins with reading. This knowledge is available to us today—as we read.

So I am vitally concerned with reading. Let us take a closer look at the actual process of reading which is thoroughly and simply described in the Book of Daniel.

> Daniel 5:7,8,15-17:
> The king cried aloud to bring in the astrologers, the Chaldeans, and the soothsayers. *And* the king spake, and said to the wise *men* of Babylon,
> Whosoever shall read this writing, and shew me the interpretation thereof, shall be clothed with scarlet, and *have* a chain of gold about his neck, and shall be the third ruler in the kingdom.
> Then came in all the king's wise *men*: but they could not read the writing, nor make known to the king the interpretation thereof.
> And now the wise *men*, the astrologers, have been brought in before me, that they should read this writing, and make known unto me the interpretation thereof: but they could not shew the interpretation of the thing:
> And I have heard of thee, that thou canst make interpretations, and dissolve doubts: now if thou canst read the writing, and make known to me the interpretation thereof, thou shalt be clothed with scarlet, and *have* a chain of gold about thy neck, and shalt be the third ruler in the kingdom.
> Then Daniel answered and said before the king, Let thy gifts be to thyself, and give thy rewards to another; yet I will read the writing unto the king, and make known to him the interpretation.

Here are five separate repetitions of the same two phases of reading. There is the matter of "reading the writing." For there is no way to "shew the interpretation thereof" without first reading the writing. However, just to read the writing is not enough. To read, as I have been using the word, one must push one's mind, the five senses of one's mind, "to shew the interpretation thereof." Interpretation is explanation. The words need to be savored, understood, until their meaning has filled the mind. That is reading. As I defined it earlier: to read is to make written words come alive in the five-senses mind so that they have the immediacy of spoken words, thus putting the reader in the presence of the speaker.

Recognizing these two phases of reading clarified much for me. You see, we can jump down to verse 25 of the same chapter, and you and I can actually read the writing:

MENE, MENE, TEKEL, UPHARSIN

Go ahead. Read it. If you have read this far, you can read these words also. Now, whether or not you pronounce them accurately, I have no way of knowing. But it says nothing here about pronouncing the words accurately. It says simply, read the writing, so who cares?

Look, we are reading Aramaic! Look, Ma, no hands. So we can read the writing. You can play "read the writing" with any unknown language written in our alphabet. Try a transliterated Greek or Hebrew text. Try a French newspaper. See, we can read the writing. But reading the writing is not all there is to reading.

There is a second equally important element: "to shew the interpretation thereof." Without this step, one is NOT reading as I am using the term in these pages. And that is why I call America an "illiterate" society today. No doubt much of the population can read the writing, BUT how many can show the interpretation thereof?

For, according to this significant passage, the true and accurate interpretation of the writing comes from God. Fortunately, it is set down for us here in verse 26-28:

> This *is* the interpretation of the thing: MENE; God hath numbered thy kingdom, and finished it.
> TEKEL; Thou art weighed in the balances, and art found wanting.
> PERES; Thy kingdom is divided, and given to the Medes and Persians.

God gave Daniel the interpretation of this writing. To understand any writing in depth, it is necessary to examine it in the light of God's Word.

So, here in this fifth chapter of Daniel, we have a simple lesson in how to read and a clear example of the two phases of reading. Benefits are stated here also. In verse 16, we find that interpretations "dissolve doubts." Now, that is a great benefit.

Also, Daniel was handsomely rewarded for carrying out the process of reading accurately. He was clothed with scarlet, a chain of gold was put about his neck, a proclamation was made that he should be the third ruler in the kingdom. Some benefits to reading! Yet, he himself told the king to keep his rewards. He had higher gains in mind.

We, too, are richly rewarded anytime we READ God's Word and shew the interpretation thereof. Like Daniel, I would gladly forego the honors for even a thimbleful, a millimeter more of enlightenment to the eyes of my understanding. For understanding of God is indeed the high prize we receive for reading accurately the Word of God. Every time we read the writing of God's Word and show the interpretation thereof, we understand more of the ways of God.

Another excellent example of the two-phase process of reading is found in Acts, chapter 8. Here in verse 27, we find a wonderful, educated man of Ethiopia, a man of influence and power. As Philip approaches, we see this great man sitting in his chariot, a scroll partly opened on his knees, revealing the Book of Isaiah. With Philip, our curiosity is piqued and we run near. What do we hear? Why, he is reading the writing.

Acts 8:30 and 31:

And Philip ran thither to *him*, and heard him read the prophet Esaias, and said, Understandest thou.what thou readest?

And he said, How can I, except some man should guide me? And he desired Philip that he would come up and sit with him.

You see, the eunuch could read the writing. But he needed Philip to show him the interpretation thereof so that he could understand. To understand is to see how it applies to your life right now. Philip opened his mouth, taught the eunuch about Jesus Christ and showed him how to apply the words to his life now. The eunuch saw and understood, for he acted on his understanding and was born again, according to verses 36-38.

Through the Word of God, as the scripture says, we have been given "all things that *pertain* unto life and godliness." The Word of God even elucidates for us what reading is and how to read. God is always so richly thorough in all that He sets before our understanding. God shows us another simple and common analogy of reading. In Jeremiah 15:16, we read:

> Thy words were found, and I did eat them; and thy word was unto me the joy and rejoicing of mine heart: for I am called by thy name, O Lord God of hosts.

God's words were found, and the man of God, Jeremiah, "did eat them." This is not a literal truth but a figure of speech which marks the process for our thoughtful scrutiny. He did not literally eat pages with words on them. He "read and digested," one might say, the reading material those words presented.

So reading and assimilating the material read are compared to the eating of food and the digestive process. Again and again throughout God's Word we find simple, concrete comparisons from everyday life used to clarify intangible and abstract processes (for example, God and His people compared to father and children; God's people compared to a building; a believer compared to a tree; God seen in terms of human body parts and emotions—the examples are profuse).

Jeremiah describes receiving, retaining and releasing mentally in terms of eating and digestion. Eating is something we are all familiar with. What happens when we eat? We close our teeth and jaws over a bite of food and chew for awhile, thus breaking down its given form. When thoroughly broken down into smaller particles, the food is swallowed. In the stomach and intestines, this bite of food is further broken down by gastric juices and movement until it is in a form that can be readily absorbed into the body by osmosis. All nutritional (profitable) elements are absorbed by the body and through "fearful and wonderful" processes, are converted into the body itself as potential energy—to run, move, think, speak. This energy moves the body physically, mentally and spiritually. Without such energy released by the ingestion of food, the body could not move and would eventually die.

In the course of digestion, nutritional elements are separated from useless elements. As the nourishing material is assimilated, the profitless accumulates in the colon and is eliminated from the body.

I have traced ingestion–digestion–elimination in some detail so we can follow through the comparison step-by-step in the matter under discussion. For the theme at hand is not physical digestion, but reading, or mental digestion. The mental process is harder to follow because it is not observable physically and to a great degree it is intangible. Yet God has set the figure here to provoke our thoughtful attention.

Jeremiah must have read the writing. That is as imperative as taking a bite of food to launch it into one's digestive system. So he read some writing—a paragraph? a verse? a sentence? pages and pages? We do not know. He must have "chewed" this writing in the forefront of his mind, considering it deeply with stayed-mind concentration so that the words had impact on his mind. An interpretation must have been shown thereof. He "swallowed" those words—took them to heart, the heart of his mind.

Then something similar to gastric juices and movements must have gone to work in the deeper recesses of Jeremiah's mind to assimilate the words. Words we read and hear do not fall into a vacuum but into our mental "innards," consisting of all our experiences, memories and other information. Through the "digestion" of our mental processes, new information becomes integrated into our own soul. It is stored there in relation to our knowledge of God's Word and to all of our experience. When assimilated, the new information then fits into our lives.

As we read further, we see that after Jeremiah "ate" these words, he had both immediate satisfaction (they were unto him the joy and rejoicing of his heart) and a longer term profit, since this food gave him energy to continue walking with God and speaking God's Word to His people.

This comparison of reading to digestion is not an isolated example. It is used again when God talks to Ezekiel, another man of God.

Ezekiel 2:8-10;3:1-4:

But thou, son of man, hear what I say unto thee; Be not thou rebellious like that rebellious house: open thy mouth, and eat that I give thee.

And when I looked, behold, an hand *was* sent unto me; and, lo, a roll of a book *was* therein;

And he spread it before me; and it *was* written within and without: and *there was* written therein lamentations, and mourning, and woe.

Moreover he said unto me, Son of man, eat that thou findest; eat this roll, and go speak unto the house of Israel.

So I opened my mouth, and he caused me to eat that roll.

And he said unto me, Son of man, cause thy belly to eat, and fill thy bowels with this roll that I give thee. Then did I eat *it*; and it was in my mouth as honey for sweetness.

And he said unto me, Son of man, go, get thee unto the house of Israel, and speak with my words unto them.

What a tremendous explication on reading! Lest we get carried away with the comparison, in Ezekiel 3:10 God gives us the explanation literally, not figuratively, so we know exactly what He is talking about:

> Moreover he said unto me, Son of man, all my words that I shall speak unto thee receive in thine heart, and hear with thine ears.

Remember our definition of reading? Reading is to make written words come alive in one's mind, so that they then become as spoken words with the same immediacy, dynamism and power as though the reader were face to face with the speaker. God wants Ezekiel *to hear* His words, hear with his ears.

As a result of ingesting the words and receiving them in the heart of his mind, Ezekiel speaks God's Word. What else would he speak? We cannot help but speak out and act out what is in our minds. So if God's Word has been read, really read, as the Scriptures present reading, we shall be unable, literally unable, to do other than to speak and to do His Word. So the real work of the renewed mind walk must be in this exact area that I am so concerned with here—how to get the Word in the mind.

Now reading the Word is a necessary first step to assimilating it into the mind. Notice that Ezekiel says, "So I opened my mouth, and he [God] caused me to eat that roll" (Ezekiel 3:2). God caused him to understand the words.

In the Gospel period, according to Luke 24, when the risen Christ appears in his resurrected body to his unbelieving disciples, he shares the Word with them, and then in verse 45:

Then opened he their understanding, that they might understand the scriptures.

The resurrected Christ opened their understanding of the written Word, the Scriptures. In our administration, Christ is seated at God's right hand, and each of us has Christ in us. Today, that Christ in us opens our understanding so we may understand the Scriptures. What will God not do through the living Christ in us to help us assimilate His Word into the hearts of our lives? Ah, He works in us. He works with us. But our part of the bargain is to read, to read, to read His Word! Give Him the chance to open your understanding.

I am so emphatic on this point, no doubt, because I need to hear this very exhortation myself again and again. We seem always to speak those things which we ourselves need to hear. I hope this detailed exploration of reading from the Word of God has clarified much for you and inspired you as well.

Now let me share with you a not uncommon phenomenon. I sit down. I pick up God's Word. I open it and begin to read. My eyes race or walk from word to word, line to line. I am reading the writing. I put down the book. What have I read? I cannot tell you. There was not one word for which I needed the dictionary. I know the meaning of the words. Yet, I have not invested that stayed-mind concentration in my reading which results in "shewing the interpretation thereof." I have not allowed the words to engage my mind.

Yes, this still happens to me occasionally. And it is with profound understanding that I hear the words of II Corinthians 3:14-16:

But their minds were blinded: for until this day remaineth

> the same vail untaken away in the reading of the old testa-
> ment; which *vail* is done way in Christ.
> But even unto this day, when Moses is read, the vail is
> upon their heart.
> Nevertheless when it shall turn to the Lord, the vail shall
> be taken away.

How I relate to this situation! Notice that these people were reading the Word. They were reading the
writing, but their minds were blinded (not actively
engaged with the words they were reading so that the
words could be assimilated into their hearts). Yes, this
veil is at times familiar to me also when I read. But
note, the solution is right there: when they turn their
heart to the Lord, the veil shall be taken away.

Set that stayed-mind concentration on God's
presence in Christ in you. Believe as you read that you
shall hear God's voice. Believe He speaks to you
through His Word, that He shall do all He can to make
those written words come alive in your mind in all their
brilliance, depth and accuracy. God is faithful.

At other moments, when my mind is balking like
some stubborn mule, when I read and do not seem able
to stay my mind to actively receive, I recall John 6:63
where Jesus states:

> It is the spirit that quickeneth; the flesh profiteth nothing:
> the words that I speak unto you, *they* are spirit, and *they*
> are life.

No matter what I feel (or do not feel) at any given
moment when I pick up the Book to read, God's words
are spirit and they are life. His words are quick. His
words are powerful. They in themselves have power to
work. I set this great truth boldly into my mind.

Whether or not I *feel* the words working does not matter. The words have power; they work whether I feel it or not.

And I bring back to mind the great record from I Samuel 5 and smile. Israel and the Philistines are at war, and Israel is on the losing end at this point. The Philistines capture the ark of the covenant. The ark contained the Word of God. The ark was the symbol of God's presence with His people. The ark was the heart of Israel, God's Word. Far worse for Israel than the capture of a flag, or of a major city, or even the king, the capture of the ark was much like stealing God from His people. What demoralization, discouragement and unbelief this theft caused among God's people!

The Philistines took the ark and brought it into the house of Dagon, their main god, and set it beside Dagon.

> I Samuel 5:3 and 4:
> And when they of Ashdod arose early on the morrow, behold, Dagon *was* fallen upon his face to the earth before the ark of the Lord. And they took Dagon, and set him in his place again.
> And when they arose early on the morrow morning, behold, Dagon *was* fallen upon his face to the ground before the ark of the Lord; and the head of Dagon and both the palms of his hands *were* cut off upon the threshold; only *the stump of* Dagon was left to him.

Look at this! Here was the Word of God in the midst of unbelief. There was no believing man with the ark to act upon God's Word. His Word was there alone. But its presence alone was enough to smite the unbelief, to cast down the idol. Its presence alone smote the

ON READING / 135

unbelievers with hemorrhoids so that they were so uncomfortable that they, posthaste, returned the ark of
God to the children of Israel, along with jewels of gold
as an apology offering!

God's Word is powerful. God's Word works even in
the midst of unbelief! For God protects and keeps His
Word. God makes His Word to work, in spite of us
sometimes. To receive the full impact and humor of
this dynamic account, read it for yourself in I Samuel
chapters 5 and 6.

This record reminds me that God's Word has immediate power, producing results even when the veil
over my heart seems so thick that I cannot hear the
Word I read.

So I confront my mind firmly, but graciously, and
say something like: "OK, OK. So you don't feel like
it. It's not coming alive. But remember, God's words
are quick and powerful whether you feel it at this moment or not. They will work. They will dissolve
doubts. They will smite your unbelief. Go ahead. Let
God's Word do the work for you. Now, you just go
ahead and read. Read." And I read anyway. What can
a mind answer back to such a reasonable and
diplomatic approach?

Looking at a printed page, I see it as a wall—tall,
neatly built, brick upon brick, word upon word. And
behind this wall, just on the other side, is a vast
land—with rivers, mountains, green valleys, cities,
plowed fields and blooming orchards; with winds and
rains and sunny days; and with people, wonderful, living people who run and laugh and weep, who wring
their hands, who love and hate, shout and whisper, and

eat, and spit into fires; people who don't understand, and then they do; people who grow and change, who commit stupidities and sometimes perform courageous and generous acts—wonderful, wonderful people populate this teeming, beautiful land.

To this land I long to fly, to run, so exciting and interesting it is, full of surprises, delicacies, details. Remember, the brain is unable to distinguish between an experience vividly imagined and an actual experience. The mind cannot tell the difference. When we read and vividly imagine it, that experience is REAL to us! We can dwell in this land. We can walk side by side with Moses, hear his resonant basso intone, "Let my people go," right under our very ears. We can sit side by side with David, hear him pluck his harp, hear him actually composing a psalm, surrounded by the aroma of rich, green, growing grass, and in the distance the occasional, comforting bleat of a sheep. We can sit very close to Jesus himself in the stillness of dawn by the blue water of Lake Galilee. We can hear his gentle voice. Let these words be imbedded in your consciousness. We can reach out our own right hand and taste for ourselves a piece of freshly broiled fish, cooked by the Master himself! It is in our very own hand, warm, crisp, delicious. We are there. We can dwell in this land.

We can follow step by meticulous step the inner workings of the mind, the very thoughts of the man of God, Paul, from Romans through Thessalonians.

That page of writing before you is a wall. Behind it, the land. Go ahead. Jump over the wall. The only way, the ONLY way, to dwell in that land is to jump over the wall. Read the writing—jump over the wall. Enter the land and take your time in the company of its wonderful inhabitants. Watch them closely. Listen for their anguish, their joys, their indecisions. Even now, they are there in the land.

The land is always there, but you can enter it only by reading the writing, by jumping over the wall. And every time you do, the dwellers of the land are still there. They never reject or expel you. You can be a part of their lives anytime, by your own decision.

Come, let us dwell together in this magnificent place. Let us invest our lives in its wonderful people. All we need do is to read the writing. Come, jump over the wall.

Essay Three

On Writing

I love to read. Surely, I am not the only one among God's people. I love to read the Word, and I love also to read other books—poetry, novels, biographies, essays, articles, memoirs. Reading helps me think. Yet, so many of the thousands of titles that are published every year are not only badly written, but also full of such error that they are hardly worth my time. And published these works are—in bulk.

Perhaps because of my own need to read, I have a vision. I walk into a library. The walls are lined with shelves, and the shelves are full of books—books of poetry, of essays, of memoirs and autobiographies, books on cooking and raising children, books of children's literature, dramas to be played and novels, yes, even novels. Books that comfort, exhort and inspire, books that teach photography and raising peonies and horse care. And they are all books written by believers in the accuracy of God's Word, books that teach principle unembellished by hot-air nonsense. These books, written from the standpoint that God's Word is truth, help to renew the mind, inspire with godly ideas and show the reader new, untapped areas of the Word's application in his life. Such is my vision of Word-centered literature. I fairly drool when I allow my mind to run with these thoughts. But before something can be read, it must be written.

If the lord returns tomorrow, I have enjoyed the edification and excitement of the vision. But if the Lord tarries for a hundred years or a thousand, why should we not avail ourselves of this form of communicating the Word of God to our children and our children's children? If the lord tarries, why not set our sights on Word-centered literature? We have nothing to lose.

Writers in the world are publishing their theories and themes. They publish because enough people out there buy their books. People buy their books because they are searching for something—perhaps a laugh, or a few moments' distraction, perhaps for knowledge in a new area, or a new idea or a better way to live. People buy books and read them. Why should the written works of our people not appear in medical and educational magazines, in libraries and private homes? If the lord tarries, why not? Surely our people, more than many others, have something worthwhile to share. Why deprive the world of this form of outreach also?

That is my vision, and if the lord tarries, there is no reason why we cannot have a growing body of literature written and published by God's people.

With this vision in mind, I share here some ideas on writing. This I know: One person will not write it all, cannot write it all. God will have to raise up many writers, specializing in many varied areas of life and research. God will have to raise up His writers, and it takes time for a writer to develop. Yet, it does not hurt to scatter seeds. Some will fall on fertile ground.

I do not know who the writers of our times will be. In accordance with my vision, I tend to see every believer I encounter as fairly bulging with at least a dozen books inside, books just waiting to be written down. I can hardly wait for these books to be done—to be available! I can hardly wait to hold them in my hands—to read, enjoy, learn, be inspired and pass them on.

So we plant some seeds, we build vision of Word-centered literature, and we reemphasize the truth that we can do it. Indeed we must do it, for the medium is available. The printing press has been invented. Books are being produced at an astonishing rate. God will open doors to make known His Word through the medium of the written word also. He is waiting for us to believe and to write them.

What is writing and what does one write? How does one write? And why write? God's Word has the answers to all these questions.

Writing must be seen in its proper context, inescapably bound with *reading* and *words*. Writing is the setting down of words which are composed of letters. Words, written words—little groupings of black marks—are the wherewithal of writing. Men write these words for other men to read at some time. They have no other purpose than to be read.

We are all writers in the broadest sense. Consider your life during the past week. Have you used written words in a letter to a friend, or in making notes on a lecture, or in jotting down some things to do, or in listing some goals? Have you perhaps made an entry in a journal, or made notes for a teaching, or written a report, or filled out a form somewhere? Hardly a day goes by without most of us writing something—that something is words. Little written words. That's all. In every instance the purpose was for these words to be read. Consider even your shopping list for the supermarket. Did you jot down a few items and then toss it out? Are you thinking: "Nobody read that. I wrote them down and then tossed the paper in the garbage."

Ah, but as you wrote down those words, you read them, and writing/reading forged those items into your memory so you could throw the list away. Perhaps *you* are the only reader of many of your written words—your journal entries, your goal lists. Perhaps you never refer to them after you have written them. But the very act of writing causes the writer to read the words. And so every word is written to be read by somebody at some time.

The body of written works is referred to as "literature," from the Latin root meaning "letters," for all written words are made up of letters. So we have the term: "a man or woman of letters," meaning a writer. Little letters combined into words are the height, depth, length and breadth of the writer's concern. How singularly dull!

Dull it may seem at a distance. But recall what was said in the previous essay, "On Reading": words have the greatest power to influence the mind. In their written form, words have a high degree of permanence and stability. So, in his intense pre-occupation with words—weighing words, choosing words, setting words down—the writer wields tremendous potential power over his own mind and the minds of others.

Those who will devote a large portion of their lives to

writing need to have an inordinate love and appreciation for words. They need to treasure them, to love and
almost adore the handling of words. For words are, in a
certain way, the world of the writer. And this world has
its immediate and long-term rewards.

As king in the kingdom of words in his mind, the
writer is absolute monarch, potentate plenipotentiary.
He controls with iron hand the words in his mind.
Words and ideas in mind are totally obedient. Do they
offend him? The writer casts them out. Does their
order displease him? He commands, and his words
scurry obediently into a new order. Strike this one!
Toss out that one! Bring in this one. Summon in a
string of others! Off with that one's head!

The realm of words in the writer's mind is a place of
awe-inspiring power. You see, words and ideas in
one's mind do not, indeed cannot, believe for
themselves. They must obey the writer's command immediately and with no talking back.

Now, the handling of people is another matter, for
people believe for themselves. One cannot order, command, demand or wipe out people with instant obe-
dience. No, people must be handled with tact, delicacy
and great sensitivity. Handling people in real life is an
extremely delicate matter.

But the power available in handling words and ideas
in the mind must have a certain measure of appeal for
the one who chooses to spend a larger portion of his life
in commanding, ordering and guiding this kingdom.

For other people, however, who devote their lives to
other ways of moving the Word, it is worthwhile to
realize the immense power they hold in their hands also

as they apply pen to paper. No matter how an individual moves God's Word, he will sooner or later write something—letters, notes, reports, etc.—in the course of his other work. In writing he has at hand the power to clarify or to confuse, to communicate or to cloud, to edify or to squelch. Ideas influence people, and words communicate ideas. The writer, whether writing in the course of other work or as his main occupation, needs to handle words with loving care and thought: an exhortation to all of us.

However, the setting down of marks on paper, even though imperative for a writer, is NOT his major work. The main work of writing is THINKING. For the words on paper to be worthy of anyone's attention, detailed thinking must precede the writing of the words. After one has thought through an idea, a poem or a story, setting it down on paper is merely the final act which must be done only after the preceding acts have been thoroughly played and replayed in the mind.

The main work of writing is thinking, and then choosing words to communicate the thoughts to the reader. There will always be a reader. Because the main work of writing is thinking, it can be vitally associated with building the Word in one's mind. Writing is a fantastic renewed mind tool for all of us—whether we aspire to become a major professional writer or not. Writing is easily accessible. Most of us already know how to write. We need very little physical paraphernalia: pen and paper. We can do it almost anywhere and at almost anytime. Writing is readily available to all of us, and the very act of writing teaches the mind to concentrate.

Having discussed the *what* of writing and having established that the main work of writing takes place in the mind, let us turn to the "how" of writing. On this the Word speaks simply and explicitly. I call Luke 1:1-4 my "writing seminar," for in these four short verses we learn what to write, how to handle our material, our attitude as writers, to whom we are writing, how to organize our material and why we write. Incredible? We shall see greater things yet.

Luke 1:1-4:

Forasmuch as many have taken in hand to set forth in order a declaration of those things which are most surely believed among us,

Even as they delivered them unto us, which from the beginning were eyewitnesses, and ministers of the word;

It seemed good to me also, having had perfect under-standing of all things from the very first, to write unto thee in order, most excellent Theophilus,

That thou mightest know the certainty of those things, wherein thou hast been instructed.

Four short verses. Note that none of the other Gospels have such a preface explaining how they came to be written. But here, preceding his account of the life of Jesus Christ, Luke (by inspiration from God) gives us the background—the what, the how and the why of its being written. It helps to answer our questions on writing today.

Verse 1:

Forasmuch as many have taken in hand to set forth in order a declaration of those things which are most surely believed among us.

What was happening? Many were attempting to set down an orderly account of "things" (*pragma*: things done, deeds, acts, matters, facts). What things? What things do we want to narrate in order? Here is the *what* of writing. What does one write? What is our material as writers? Those things most surely believed among us. Here is one vital key to our subject matter when we write. We must believe in what we write. Our material is "those things most surely believed among us." Notice that Luke, by inspiration from God, was not specific (which is why I call this my writing seminar). He did not state: "Many were attempting to set down an orderly account of the life of our lord, Jesus Christ." That would have been too specific. Although an orderly account of the life of Jesus Christ certainly falls under the heading of "those things most surely believed among us," stating the principle, rather than the specific, allows us a far broader immediate application.

Well, what are those things most surely believed among us? Digesting this question through my mind, I came up with only two broad categories. First, the obvious one—God's written Word. Is that not the basic foundation of all our beliefs?

The second broad category I call the living Word: what God has done for you in your life, what He has done for me in mine—how He called us, how He healed us, how He delivered us, comforted us, opened our understanding. Are not these also among "those things most surely believed among us"?

What then is our material as writers? Luke 1:1, "those things most surely believed among us," which fall into two broad categories: the written Word and the living Word.

With the written Word as our material, we have all

types and sizes of research writing: *The Bible Tells Me So*; *The New, Dynamic Church*; *Jesus Christ Is Not God*; these are a few examples. These take a certain theme, or point, from the written Word and expound that point with our written words. Are these not "those things most surely believed among us"?

With the living Word we have the newspaper, *Heart*, as an example—records in specific detail of God working in people's lives. Are these not also "those things most surely believed among us"?

What of poems, novels, essays, biographies? All these forms of the written Word will fall under one of these two categories. I can think of no literary form excepted from "those things most surely believed among us."

In Acts 4:20, we have a statement that adds more light to the *what* of our material as writers. Peter states very simply: "For we cannot but speak the things which we have seen and heard." We cannot but write the things which we have seen and heard, either. If I have "seen" some portion of the Word of God fit together; if I have "seen" God work in my life in a particular instance (whether I put it into poetic or novel form), these qualify as "those things most surely believed among us."

Let me add that we often have information or words in our minds that we have not proved for ourselves. Written down, these thoughts will not have as much vitality in them as some section of the Word of God that we ourselves have minutely worked or a firsthand experience we have "seen and heard" ourselves. Those things that we have "seen and heard," experienced, worked first-hand, will communicate a depth of conviction and reality available no other way.

So, we see here the *what* of our material. What we write is "those things most surely believed among us." Now how do we handle our material, whether in the written Word or the living Word category? That is clearly shown to us in Luke, chapter 1, verse 2:

> Even as they delivered them unto us, which from the beginning were eyewitnesses, and ministers of the word.

Many had written from their eyewitness accounts—their records, their research, their testimonies, their observations, their accounts of what had happened. Those, who at the time of writing were born again and in the Administration of Grace, were characterized as "eyewitnesses" AND as "ministers of the Word." How long? "From the beginning."

Now, this is a verse of tremendous insight. They handled the material as eyewitnesses and as ministers of the Word; this is our twofold approach to our material also.

What is an eyewitness? This word in the Greek is transliterated *autoptēs*, from *auto* meaning "self" and *optēs* meaning "seen"; it is "seen by oneself"—a personal observation, inspection and examination. This is a medical term that comes to us as "autopsy"—the personal oberservation, inspection and partial dissection of a dead body to learn the cause of death; a postmortem examination. These writers approached their material as eyewitnesses. This is a very minute and detailed examination of one's material, requiring acute observation, sharp senses, fastidious attention to detail.

As an approach to our material for writing today, I believe that our *autoptēs* of it, our careful scrutiny, examination and analysis of it is to pinpoint and determine the CAUSE OF LIFE, not the cause of death as in a medical autopsy.

Suppose you are writing a short piece for *The Way Magazine* on the love of God. You approach those things most surely believed among us as an *autoptēs*, an eyewitness. You personally observe, carefully inspect— yes, even partially or wholly dissect verses from the Word of God on this theme to see firsthand how they fit together, to put your finger on the pulse, the cause of life.

Or suppose you are writing an article on your Twig for *Heart*. Can you see the need to approach your material as an eyewitness, an *autoptēs*? In matters of life we have our five senses, guided by the Christ in us. You would carefully observe, examine, inspect: What was said? What did they do? What inspired the believing? What did they wear? Where did they go? How did they act? What was the feeling, the atmosphere, etc.? You would send out your most sensitive feelers to take in specific details, all to the end of determining in the situation the cause of life.

And so, whether we handle material from the written Word of God or from the living Word, we approach it as eyewitnesses. But that is not all. That word in the text is followed by an ''and'' connecting to it an equally necessary condition.

The world boasts of many keen observers of life. Such a sharp observer could come into a Twig to do a story on that Twig. He could faithfully and minutely record what he saw, heard, felt, tasted, smelled and touched in the situation. But, he would still lack the other basic ingredient necessary to approaching the material.

"And minister of the word (*logos*)." "Minister" here is transliterated from the Greek as *hupēretēs*, meaning an underrower, a common sailor; hence, any subordinate person acting under the direction of another. We as writers must be such "ministers of the word." Similarly, as we work in some other capacity to move God's Word, carrying a spiritual responsibility—as a Twig coordinator, a Limb secretary, a class coordinator, a WOW, a Way Corps member or Staff member—we gain the heart for our material that the keenest observer from the world could not possibly have.

So our approach to our material as writers is twofold. We handle it as *autoptēs*, eyewitnesses, keen observers of the detail, careful investigators, thoughtful examiners (whether we are handling the written Word or the living Word), and also we approach our material as ministers of the Word, *hupēretēs*, workers in some capacity, some responsibility, moving the Word of God.

Notice also that these two qualities are cited in Luke 1:2 as having been necessary attitudes of writers "from the beginning." They took the time to start, follow through, digest, work, live with their material. As I see it, time is involved here. They did not jump in, observe, write haphazardly. No, they worked with their material from the beginning of it straight through. As if you were writing a piece on the love of God, you would start from the beginning, the most obvious verses, perhaps, and take time to work the verses in some depth. You would work the material from the beginning to the end.

However, that is not all. For the best writing (as opposed to only good writing) includes not only being an eyewitness and minister of the Word, but also a total reliance on the spirit of God resident within us. This is what gave Luke the edge over other writers.

Verse 3 opens with the finest statement I have ever heard on one's attitude as a writer: "It seemed good to me also," he says. And if you are thinking of becoming a writer, it had better seem good to you also, a pleasure, in fact, to write. Even if you do not consider writing as a profession—if you are merely writing a letter in the course of your main occupation—it would not hurt you to have this attitude: "It seemed good to me" to write this letter, note or whatever.

I believe it must have seemed good to Moses also to sit down and write the first five books of the Bible. I bet it seemed good to David also to compose the Psalms he wrote. It must have seemed good to Paul also to write Romans, Corinthians, Galatians, etc. In fact, it must have seemed good to all the men of God who spake as they were moved by the Holy Spirit.

So much for our attitudes as writers. If it does not seem good to you, if you have no pleasure in it, forget it. You are only losing rewards, for unless it seems good to you to write, you will be outside the love and will of God. So, if we are to become writers to move the Word of God around the world, like Luke, let it seem good to us also to write.

The next phrase of verse 3 adds the other essential

aspect to the twofold approach to our material set forth in verse 2 (that of being an eyewitness *and* minister of the Word from the beginning).

Luke 1:3a:

It seemed good to me also, having had perfect understanding of all things from the very first.

He can write because he already has "perfect understanding." "Perfect" is the Greek word transliterated *akribōs*, meaning "accurate, precise, exact." "Understanding" is *parakoloutheō*, which is "to accompany side by side, to follow closely; *then*, to follow out closely *in mind*, trace out, examine" step by step.

What is this but a contrast, showing Luke as more than an eyewitness and minister. He was a spirit-filled professional. How do we exactly and accurately follow closely, and then follow closely in mind, but by being keen observers, eyewitnesses of the specifics and by being spirit-filled ministers of the Word of God in some capacity? We discern spiritually, but God expects us to know what we can by our five senses.

In your short article for *The Way Magazine* on the love of God, would you not accurately, precisely and exactly gather together the verses on the love of God in the Word? Would you not follow them through closely in your mind, dwell on them, sift through them, trace them out in the Word, so you would truly be an eyewitness and minister of the Word?

Or, as an example of writing in the category of the living Word, suppose you are writing an article on Dr. Wierwille preparing for an Advanced Class. Would you not *follow him*, precisely, exactly, accurately listening for every word, observing his acts? And then, might you not also follow through exactly and accurately in your mind all the material you had, sifting, weighing, looking for significance?

We gain a Godly perspective by approaching our material from the beginning as eyewitnesses and ministers of the Word, keeping our ears tuned to the spirit of God. We must be diligent, faithful, precise and honest, but the whole responsibility does not rest mercilessly upon us. God is our Co-worker. God is in Christ in us day and night without sleep or slumber. God works in us both to will and to do of His good pleasure.

The next phrase is "of all things from the very first." "Very first" is a poor translation of the Greek word *anōthen*, and this is the only place it is so translated. In other places it is rendered "from above." The most frequent context shows it to mean *by revelation* from God. (Examples: John 3:31; 19:11; James 1:17; 3:15,17.) So the "perfect understanding" of all things (pertaining to the subject, *pasin*, meaning "all things, *as constituting a whole*") comes from above, from God through the Christ in you.

Look, this is so accurate, I am astonished! Our minds and senses are phenomenal (fearfully and wonderfully made)! The information we can observe, gather and store is amazing. There is no way art can imitate life. Life is life, and art is art, and writing is writing. Art in general, and writing in particular, can present only a limited portion of life for careful scrutiny. God knows this too. Look at John 21:25:

> And there are also many other things which Jesus did, the which, if they should be written every one, I suppose that

even the world itself could not contain the books that should be written. Amen.

Amen to that! Writing does not cover *everything*. It cannot. The world has no room for all the books it would take. God says so Himself. As keen eyewitnesses and ministers of the Word over a period of time, following through some aspect of research in the written Word of God or of the Word living in God's people today, we will have such a formidable plethora of information on the cause of life that we would be thoroughly knowledgeable but utterly confused by all the detail, but for this wonderful truth:

The perfect understanding of all things comes *anōthen*, from above. God is working through Christ in us. As we apply ourselves to our material, the Christ in us will show us what is important and valuable to include. Everything is too much, is impossible, but *anōthen*, from above, we will see the specific detail, the particular points to bring out.

Perhaps an article you write on the love of God will center on tying together three verses on this theme. There must be hundreds in the Word of God. But as you honestly follow them through accurately from the beginning and then follow through accurately in your mind, the material to emphasize will be revealed to you through Christ in you. God knows who will read your article, what would bless them the most. As you follow through your material accurately in your mind, the Christ in you brings you to a "perfect understanding of all things," and you narrow down your article to three main verses, or one main point. How can we as writers go wrong with such loving power at work within us?

So, we have seen what our material is, how to approach it, our attitude as writers and how the process works. We have seen what we are responsible to do and what God through Christ in us will do, for we are co-workers together with Him.

Fine. Now, how do we write it? How do we organize this material? Good question, since we have our material together and have worked it closely in mind.

The next phrase in Luke 1:3 tells us exactly how: "to write unto thee in order." IN ORDER—that is how we organize our material. In order. The word "order" is transliterated *kathexēs* (*kata* meaning "according to," and *hexēs*, "order *or* succession, consecutively, in a connected order"). To learn more specifics on order, we may take the Word of God as an example. What order does God use? Well, He starts from the beginning for one thing: Genesis 1:1, "In the beginning God...."

In His Word, God often uses a chronological order, at other times He does not. But in all instances, God's Word exemplifies ORDER—logical, simple order.

Of all the art forms, the written Word has the greatest blessing and concomitant responsibility, for we have a concrete example of our form—written words. We can search out direct examples of usage, structure, form, setting, theme, characterization, imagery, style, etc. Those involved in other fields of art (architecture, theatre, dance, visual arts, music, etc.) do not have an actual, concrete example of something done by the hand of artists to hold forth His Word in other art forms. These forms will have to be worked out from the principles of writing which are directly exemplified in God's written Word.

Let me digress from our general theme of order here and explain exactly what I mean. Any written word, literature, is a form for communicating ideas. Within the form of the written word are many more specific forms. A poem and a biography, an essay and a novel are very different in specific form even though they all are literature. Why use one or another form? That is an excellent question.

God's Word contains an excellent example of every possible specific form the written word can take. God, the master Author, has given us an example of every possible literary form. We can study and decide, directly from God's Word, exactly what form of writing we want to use.

A novel, for example, has three main elements. First, a novel has a *main character*, introduced early in the work. Second, the main character is immediately faced with a *problem*. Perhaps he goes off to seek his fortune, or he is convinced there must be more meaning to life and has determined to find it. Or, like Ulysses, perhaps his problem is how to get home now that the war is over. Any kind of problem will do, but the main character must face a problem early in the work.

The body of the novel is the record of the main character dealing with his problem. He confronts hindrances and obstacles; his character (his willingness and ability) is revealed. In a secular novel, some obstacles and hindrances will baffle, some will overcome him. Others cause him to be original, courageous, brave. In any case, his weaknesses and strengths show themselves as he handles the problem. And so his character is revealed.

Finally, the problem is *resolved*, the third element necessary to a novel. The resolution can take many forms: He may find his answer and ride off into the sunset. He may finally come home. He may find there is not a greater meaning to life, that his quest was in vain. Or he can die.

Main character, problem, resolution—these are the three basic elements of a novel.

Now, let us look at the Bible. It opens with a main character: "In the beginning God...." Immediately, the main character is confronted with a problem— Adam's disobedience. The body of the work is the record of the main character dealing with the problem in the face of obstacles and hindrances that reveal His character (His willingness and His ability). Finally, the problem is completely resolved in the Book of Revelation—every detail and facet of the problem is resolved. Isn't that wonderful? The Word of God as a whole is the greatest example of the structure of the novel. I believe it is the archetype—the original—on which all other novels are modeled structurally.

Now, an autobiography follows the general structure of a novel, but the author is the main character, talking about or revealing himself. In the Word of God the author reveals Himself! The whole Word of God may be seen as an autobiography.

An essay is the systematic and logical development of a series of ideas upon a given theme. Emerson, one of the world's greatest essayists, writes about "Friendship," for example. He does not bring in horsebreeding or hybrid roses. No, his theme is friendship, so he systematically and logically lays out in order, so the reader can follow, his ideas on friendship.

Essays used to bore me, for I missed in them the action of a novel, of characters laughing, crying, making love. I thought essays lacked people. But no, I was wrong. The main character is very present in the essay, for therein are his very thoughts, the most intimate workings of his mind. He lays bare *his* ideas, the heart of his thoughts. How much more closely can one be involved with another person than to know the logical and systematic development of his thoughts upon a given theme? "For as he thinketh in his heart, so *is* he" (Proverbs 23:7a). This is what the essay form presents.

Now, God had the whole Word of God in His foreknowledge. He "thought the whole thing through." He had to wait for men to rise up, believe and write down these thoughts of His. But if the Word was in God's foreknowledge, His thinking, then the whole Word might be termed an essay, the logical and systematic development of the author's ideas upon a given theme.

A poem is also a form of written words. Poetry places additional limitations on the writer, and these are the main qualities which set it apart from other forms of writing. Usually the limitation will be a rhyme scheme or rhythm pattern—or both. The author does not simply state his idea, or image, but he structures it within a certain recognizable pattern. Poems are characterized by an absolute economy of language. Every single word counts.

Now, we know from God's Word that He knows more than His Word (Deuteronomy 29:29). He has other knowledge. The revealed Word is not all He knows or all His ideas. So He deliberately imposed on Himself a particular literary pattern. He exemplified absolute economy of language. There is a purpose for how, when, where, to whom and why every word is used. God Himself stands behind every jot and tittle. No other word, at any given place, would do. So, we might look at the whole written Word of God as a poem—a Father's poem for His people—in literary form.

God's Word as a whole can be seen as a novel, an autobiography, an essay and a poem. What secular literary work exemplifies such diversity of form in one work? From a literary point of view, the Bible must be God's Word. No man has ever, indeed, could ever think things through so thoroughly, so simply and so accurately.

Let us look now within the Word of God. Within the Bible, examples of every possible literary form can be discovered and studied by us—aspiring writers who ask ourselves such questions as: How does God use various literary forms? Why this form at this place? How are they structured, etc.?

Do you want an example of a short story? Look at the Book of Ruth, the Book of Esther. How about drama? The Book of Job, the Song of Solomon. How about poetry? Any of the Psalms. How about a song? Try the song of Moses (Deuteronomy 31) or Deborah's song (Judges 5). Are you looking for biography? How does God handle the life of Abraham, or the life of Moses, or Samuel, or David? Surely, these are biographies. How about history? Look at Chronicles. How about journalism or actuality (a writer reporting his observations of people, actions, places)? Look at the four Gospels. Matthew, Mark, Luke and John were excellent journalists.

Do you want scenario, screenplay? Try the Book of Acts. Literally, this book is laid out with the camera shots—pans, follow shots, close-ups—and dialogue. How about essay—the systematic and logical development of a person's ideas upon a given theme? Look at the Church Epistles and at Hebrews.

To clarify the difference between journalism and essay, consider the Gospel of Luke and Corinthians, side by side. What do we know about Luke, the man, from the Gospel of Luke? Of course, we are hearing his vocabulary, but we do not know much of how he feels. He is recording the people, events, happenings of that time, particularly the life, death and resurrection of Jesus Christ. This type of writing is journalism, or actuality— what happened as observed (spiritually or physically) by the writer.

But what do we know about Paul from Corinthians? Ah, so much! We know what caused him to weep, what brought him joy and anguish. We know where he went, how he dealt with people, how God worked specifically with him. We know his relationship to the people he mentions, whom he baptized, whom he held dear.

Essays are sprinkled with personal incidents from the life of the writer. These always build the reader's believing to receive the writer's ideas on the theme. So in the epistles of Paul, the innermost, intimate depths of the heart of the man of God for our administration are laid down to be followed step by step by the reader. Through Paul's epistles we are not only walking beside him, eating with him, watching him, listening to him (journalism), but also we are in the dynamic center of his thoughts, following the workings of his heart—the heart of the man speaking for God in this Administration of Grace.

Another example of a literary form is the Book of Revelation. This book foretells the future accurately as God revealed to John what will really happen. Science fiction, I believe, is the counterfeit of foretelling the future accurately. Science fiction speculates on the future, in most instances, from man's point of view.

The Word has examples of fable, where nonhuman objects, such as trees, talk. In I Corinthians 12, parts of the human body talk together. There are examples also of parable, the bare bones of the short story and novel forms.

The literary forms and examples of them we have discussed are those that I have so far spotted. I am convinced there are others, many others. Here is a wealth, an open field for inquiry and study in God's Word: the Word of God as literature, tracing and studying its various literary forms, their structure, style, characterization, setting, imagery, theme, historical background, etc. But these examples serve to show our privilege and responsibility as writers in having a concrete (and perfect) example of art from which to learn.

We cannot observe firsthand Noah's ark or the Temple or the New City (although we can read about them all) to have a tangible example of God-inspired architecture and shipbuilding. We cannot observe a God-inspired dance in the Bible, even though it is written that various people danced by inspiration from God at various times. We cannot hear the music of God-inspired musicians and composers of Bible times, even though we know they sang and played music—all to move the Word. We cannot study firsthand the sculpture, stonecutting, gem setting, weaving of the Bible's God-inspired professionals. We know only that believers produced in all areas of art and culture. But in literature we have an actual, concrete work to study and imitate. That is why writers have such a great privilege and responsibility. Having the Word of God before us, we have no excuse to fall short.

Furthermore, I believe the principles we can learn about from God's Word and apply in writing are translatable into other art forms to communicate the Word of God more effectively in our day and time.

This major (and I hope inspiring) digression has been to shed light on our question of HOW we write and God's simple answer: "in order." Once I know to write "in order," the next question is very obvious: what order? So we have discussed various approaches to order by looking at examples of literary forms in God's Words.

Now, how are the literary principles of order translatable into other art forms?

An incident occurred recently in which two painters were discussing how to organize a painting. One maintained that first priority was to define the planes in space on the canvas (the depth). Second, he maintained, was to mark in the major horizontals and verticals, which are the "unmovables." Third was to work out the movable objects, which can be moved around within the unmovable structure for balance. The other painter agreed that the movables came last but insisted that one must first put in the verticals and horizontals (the "unmovables") and then mark the planes in space (depth) later.

Because these two painters were believers, they went to the Word of God for answers. Genesis chapter 1 gives us a divine point of comparison. What did God do? How did He establish order? First He said, "Let there be light." Now, light gives depth, or planes in space. Where there is no light, there is no depth of space. When He said, "Let there be light," He was defining depth of space.

Next, He established order among the large, stable objects, the unmovables: heavens and earth, sun, moon and stars. Are these not the basic horizontals and verticals? Finally, He included His smaller, movable elements—plants, animals, man.

Is that not wonderful? Isn't it so simple, once seen? God surely knows the best, the simplest, the most efficient order in which to do a work. Should we not seriously learn from His example in our own works?

As this conversation was recounted to me, I was, of course, applying the order to my field, writing. If I am writing a novel, a poem, an essay, the first thing to be established is the theme—how deep shall I go? How much light shall be revealed? First, I must define the planes in space—the depth. ("Let there be light.") Second, the "unmovables," the horizontals and verticals, must be decided. In writing, this includes decisions on the form, and with that, the setting, the time period, the point of view. Finally, the "movables" are set in the context of the "unmovables." The "movables" can be changed around. One incident or another may be substituted to reveal a character in a novel—but the characters, story and setting are all stable, calculated to make known the theme (light).

God's order of doing a work, as set forth in Genesis 1, is a standard for comparison to every type of human activity. Since God did it this way, this sequence must be the best order of doing anything. And it is simple.

Now, let us return to our major study on how to write, from Luke 1:1-4. We were discussing order. How do we write? We write in order, starting from the beginning. The order is simple, logical, for the mind works in a linear pattern and is able to give its fullest attention to only one thought at a time.

Now, to whom do we write? This question so puzzled me when I was working on *The Way: Living in Love*, that I literally spent months weighing it in my mind. Was I writing to an audience in the world, or to the believers already born again? If to the former, I would have to take time to explain all specialized words (e.g., prophecy, tongues, etc.).

Luke 1:3 gives direction. We write to edify the Body of Christ. "...Most excellent Theophilus"—Luke is addressing the believers. Theophilus is "beloved of God." The title "most excellent" (*kratistē*) is a title used in addressing persons of rank and authority, as an ambassador from a foreign country today might be addressed as "Your Excellency." It is a term of high respect.

In this address I see the attitude we as writers need to hold toward our audience. We hold them in high regard, high esteem. We treasure their hearts, their time. We work our writing to be the most edifying and polished. The reader to whom we write is the believer (or potential believer) whom we esteem very highly. We are concerned with his edification.

The Bible was written for believers. The unbelievers will never believe it anyway. We write to edify the Body of Christ. Here is a place to be spiritually and practically sharp.

The world consists of only two kinds of people: believers and unbelievers. God in His foreknowledge knows all who will believe. He already calls them His own, in Romans 4:17:

(As it is written, I have made thee a father of many nations,) before him whom he believed, *even* God, who quickeneth the dead, and calleth those things which be not as though they were.

Some of these "believers" that God already knows do not know yet that they are called of God. Many of us can remember a time when we were "rank unbelievers." Yet all that time—and from before the foundation of the world—God knew us to be believers. So now, as you write, you are writing to edify the Body of Christ. But, on any occasion of writing you need to be aware of your particular audience and tailor your vocabulary to that audience. Our pupose in writing is always to be understood, so we use vocabulary appropriate to our specific audience.

Suppose you are writing children's literature. It is essential to choose words and ideas geared to the particular age-group for whom you are writing. Suppose, on the other hand, you are a doctor or a nurse writing an article on some particular point in your field. Your vocabulary needs to be tailored to your readers. The truth, accuracy and love of your presentation, however, would even bless someone like me, who knows nothing of your field. At the same time, such a presentation, even if it's on techniques of tying knots in surgery, could attract a believer who does not yet know he is a believer.

Really, the principle is simple. We speak in wisdom, just as when we are witnessing. We choose a vocabulary and illustrations that will be easily received by the particular hearer. So also in writing. Some of our writings, being evangelical in nature (this is, purposed to draw the believer who does not yet know he is a believer), will be couched in a vocabulary understandable to our particular audience, yet our purpose is always to build up the Body of Christ in love.

And now to the why of writing. Why write? This question is answered in Luke 1:4:

> That thou mightest know the certainty of those things, wherein thou has been instructed.

"That" introduces the purpose or design and might be paraphrased "in order that." "Thou" is the person he is addressing, Theophilus, the beloved of God, the believer. In order that the believer (that's you and me today) might know (not doubt, not question, not wonder, but KNOW), *epignōs* (to know fully, well, thoroughly), the certainty, (*asphaleian*—steadfastness, firmness, stability) of those things (*logōn*, words) wherein "thou hast been instructed." This final word is *katēchēthēs*, to sound forth towards anyone, hence, to teach, especially orally or by preaching.

Did we not all hear the accuracy of God's Word in a class called Power for Abundant Living? Was not the Word (*logōn*) taught (*katēchēthēs*) orally to us? Yes, and then we all strode into life with a miraculously renewed mind, never confused, never wavering, right? No! The renewed mind takes time to work, to develop, to experience. So we read *The Bible Tells Me So* and reread and reread. And does that reading and rereading not help us to KNOW the certainty of those things wherein we had been instructed in the Power for Abundant Living class?

How about an article in *The Way Magazine* or in *Heart*—does that not reiterate, reemphasize for our constantly fading in-and-out minds the certainty of those things wherein we were instructed? Why, of course!

This also is why we write today. We write "those things most surely believed among us" in the written or the living Word of God. When readers read they know again, more deeply, and see with greater clarity and conviction the certainty of those things wherein they have been instructed, that is : the accuracy and integrity of God's matchless Word.

So, I have called these four verses in Luke a veritable seminar on how to write. In these verses all our questions are answered: what to write, how to handle material, how to organize, our attitudes as writers, to whom we write and why. How economical and profitable a few written words can be!

I had read these verses many times before I recognized the instruction on writing in them. I believe I was able to recognize them as such when my understanding and grasp of the scope of God's Word had finally grown to where I could spiritually see the instruction. But also because from my experience as a writer I knew the problems a writer must handle. Some of these same conclusions I had already drawn, after years of trial and error in the writing field. And I was still not absolutely certain I was right. How much simpler it would have been for me if someone had shown me this simple instruction on how to write. A winding path of trial and error could have been avoided. But I thank God that you, the aspiring writer, can start from here today.

At PFAL '77, I had occasion to work with ten writers during two weeks. Having shared this instruction with them at the beginning of our working time, I was blessed and amazed to see the results. Most of them were novices in the writing field. But they believed God's Word. In two to three days some of them were producing a quality of material it had taken me years to attain, because their basic questions on what, how and why had been answered at the onset.

Now, instruction has been given, but let me hasten to point out here that instruction alone does not make a writer. The writer develops by applying the instruction himself. The only way to learn to write, and more, to learn to write well, is to do it. Do it and continue doing it. Like our walk with God, like believing or eating, no one else can do it for you. You must do it for yourself. In writing, you must continue over a period of time.

Keep in mind, however, that any kind of writing is writing and therefore falls under the category of practice. Whether you are writing letters to WOWs, to friends, to disgruntled parents or children, whether you are keeping notes of teachings, keeping a journal or diary, whether you are writing a memo, a report or filling out a form, you are writing. Every bit of practice with awareness of the the use of your words helps you to better communicate with words on paper. Take advantage of the writing opportunities that daily come your way, and consider your words.

*   *   *

Several times in my life I have had occasion to work as a simultaneous interpreter—Russian/English, German/English. This work struck me as so similar to the process of writing that I would like to share this comparison here.

There you are, standing alongside of two people. They are educated, literate, full of ideas. But, because they do not speak the same language, they cannot possibly understand one another. Their only hope for communication is through an interpreter—you.

One of them speaks. You listen very intently, trying not to miss a nuance or implication in the choice of words used. Your mind races through a dozen possibilities of how to put these words in the other language. Boldly you begin to say the things spoken, translated into the other language. No one can check on you, because the two for whom you are interpreting cannot know how accurate you are. You are on your own.

Even though you, the interpreter, are absolutely vital to the conversation, you are like a machine, a telephone, and are hardly noted for yourself. In fact, the times you are noticed are only those times that you make an obvious mistake. You pause to reach for a word which eludes you. The conversation stops abruptly. All eyes glare questioningly at you, as your stomach squirms. But such mistakes are few. Mostly, the conversation between the two main parties continues smoothly. You are not even noticed. The conversation continues through the translation of words in your brain.

Mentally, simultaneous interpretation is intense and exhausting activity. Listening in one language, mentally translating into several possibilities, and then speaking out one alternative is such mentally demanding work that there is not one iota of mental space to give a thought to how your feet hurt, or how hungry you are, or how dumb the conversation is.

Intense concentration on what is happening and holding the words of two languages in the mind is totally absorbing. But the process allows two people who otherwise could not understand each other, to communicate with each other. As interpreter, you receive input, translate into other words, and produce output.

I think thus of the process of writing also. In a writing situation my input is all I can receive through my five senses (led by the holy spirit). As a writer, I think of myself as a five-senses sponge. Seeking to absorb with intense concentration, I look and see, listen intently and hear. I smell, taste, feel and touch all that I can in that situation. But all the time I push my mind to translate these sensations, these impressions, the details of the sights, sounds, smells, feelings, tastes into words, words, words.

*   *   *

It is amazing to me that I find myself going through life not noticing detail! I could have an intense conversation with someone, walk away and ask myself: What color were that person's eyes, or hair? What was he wearing? How did that person move? What was the tone of his voice? Sonorous, low, tense? Walking away from such a conversation, not ten minutes later, I gasp in disbelief, laughing. I do not remember! I cannot answer those questions! I am amazed at my lack of awareness in such instances.

But in any situation, let the thought once pass through my mind: If I were going to write about this, what would I say? Suddenly, my senses and mind leap to alertness. The scene bursts alive with vivid details. The eyes are green, greyish green, and soft. Soft but firm. Green, the color of olive leaves. The skin is smooth, dark, with hardly a hint of wrinkles. The body is at ease, moving only to emphasize a word spoken. The voice low, sonorous, throaty even, but in a pleasing manner. The clothes, the surroundings, all come alive when I set my mind to translate sensations and impressions into words.

On these occasions, when I walk away, my mind is buzzing with details already translated into WORDS. Should I choose to sit down and record the occasion, I already have a vast store of words—words from which I may choose the most accurate and vivid ones.

Suppose that particular conversation was an interview. Having pushed the "come-alive" button that sets my mind to translating details into words, I can then sit down later and write it. You, the reader, at some later time sit down and read—really read—that record. If I have done my job as a writer and you read the account, then you are face to face with the person yourself. You see, hear and are aware of a person or situation you could never have experienced except through the writer's written words. You are there (though you were not there literally) by reading the writer's written words. The writer has "interpreted"—input from his five-senses details translated into output—words written down on paper. This is why writing is so much like simultaneous interpretation to me.

Many times I do this simply to exercise my mind and build my fluency of translation into words. Try it yourself. Next time you sit at a meeting, or walk into your job, or talk with someone, place before your mind the challenge: If I were going to write about this, what would I say? And watch your surroundings come vividly alive as your mind translates impressions into words. You will find after having done this that you can easily call the entire situtation back into your mind at a later time, and the scene will be alive with details. If you want to write it then, it will be a matter of choosing the best words to convey the actuality of the situation to a reader. But having translated into many words already, you will have a wide selection of words from which to choose the most communicative.

I am confident in the results you will receive because this is a matter of principle. The greater effort put forth, the more that is received and retained. In carrying out the challenge ("If I were going to write about this, what would I say?"), you are giving forth added effort and you receive and retain more. It is a matter of principle, and I have found this a constructive mental exercise which can be carried out almost anywhere at anytime.

When I searched out the depths of *autopiēs* (eyewitness) in Luke 1:2, I thrilled at its accuracy, which I had learned through years of trial and error. For eyewitness it is—your five-senses detail input. Writing and reading are five-senses activities. Now, they may reveal spiritual matters, but they are still five-senses activities. A piece of writing needs five-senses detail to give the mind of the reader something concrete to follow.

I have seen in some of my writing and in the writing of beginners a tendency to generalize. This does not give the reader enough detail to allow the written word to come alive in his mind when he reads. He may be the most concentrated and experienced reader, but if the details are not given by the writer, the reader has nothing to latch onto mentally.

The mind is a five-senses organ. It operates in time and space. Well-chosen details, translated into words on paper, pass the time and fill the space of the reader's mind. This is the writer's responsbility.

Since we are talking about the writer's responsibility and the process of writing, let us compare writing with other art forms. A ballerina or a pianist—one who is serious—needs to spend a certain amount of his life (preferably daily) in "studio time," practicing his specialty. If he neglects to practice for awhile, a decline in technique will be noticeable. The ballerina's constant working out and the pianist's practice are necessary for technical smoothness and proficiency.

For the writer it is different. His basic "techniques"—grammar, vocabulary, writing down—are "masterable." When the writer can write down words (which most of us can do after high school), when he has mastered basic grammar and has a usable vocabulary, he does not need to practice grammar, vocabulary and penmanship. Many of us have mastered these in the course of normal education. The writer does not need "studio time" in the same sense as the ballerina or the pianist.

The writer's studio is life. His studio time must be in living, in experiencing firsthand, in getting involved so that he HAS SOMETHING TO SAY. He must live and experience AND reflect or think about it (translate into words; choose the best ones to communicate). Remember, the major work of the writer is THINK-ING. He needs to have something to think about, and that means doing things, getting involved.

Look at Moses. Raised as the son of Pharoah, forty years in the wilderness leading the children of Israel out of Egypt, more wilderness, judging, dealing with, encouraging people—that man had done a few things. He had experienced a slice of life. When he got around to it, that man had SOMETHING TO SAY.

Think of David, of Isaiah, Jeremiah, of Paul the apostle. Indeed, none of those holy men of God who spake as they were moved by the Holy Spirit were wallflowers. They were out there living, feeling, involved to their eyeballs in the business of living. When God moved them to record His Word, He had something to work with. They had something to say.

I am bringing up these examples of great writers because in our day there is such a perpetuation of the myth that the writer is a removed individual. Isolated from life, he observes everything coolly from his ivory tower. Not so in the Word of God. The writers of the Bible were the most involved men of their times. They lived life and believed God to their very marrow. They had the most to say. Let this be our standard also.

The writer's studio is life. He, more than most, needs direct involvement. Little does it matter what kind of experience. Whether he drives trucks, digs ditches, works as a mail clerk or in an office. Almost any type of work involves us with people of one kind or another, puts us in diverse situations, and all this experience can be fruitful material for writing at some time.

Let me insert here that a part of the writer's life experience may well be reading also. In fact, most writers are avid readers; many who read much find a facility in writing. Why? Because reading is dealing with words and writing is dealing with words. Reading builds stayed-mind concentration and mental facility and appreciation of words—the power of words.

In the essay "On Reading," I pointed out that writing is inescapably connected to reading and words, and that effective reading is in direct proportion to how much one has lived, how much he has experienced firsthand. For words are only symbols of things, hard to grasp if one does not know "the things" firsthand.

We know that the great writers of the Bible were readers. They read the Word, studied it, memorized it. From Moses to Jesus Christ to Paul, these men were readers, readers of the Word, in any case. What other material they read, I do not know. But they avidly read God's Word, and some developed as writers.

So let this be a standard for us also as aspiring

writers. Let us be doers, involved in life to the hilt. And let us also be readers, avid readers—of God's Word first, and also of other material—for as we read we build in our minds a stronger grasp of the utilization and appreciation of words, the very world of the writer.

Now, all of us who are alive experience something. Most of us talk about what we experience. So far, writers are like everyone else. But here is where the writer travels by a separate route. He not only lives, experiences and talks about it with others, but also he reflects (thinks actively) about his experiences. He translates those things he has seen and heard into words. And he does not stop there. Having reflected, sifted, weighed, he then carries out that final act—the act that makes him the writer. He writes his words on paper. (At this stage, I have found a certain amount of solitude and partial isolation are necessary.)

He sits down (I have found no other way to write than to sit down somewhere, preferably at a table. Writing while walking or running simply does not work for me). Carefully selecting words, he commits these words to paper. When done, he again needs involvement, people, experience, life, to have something else to say worthy of being read.

There is no way one can be a writer without finally writing something on paper. But I have found, from the Word of God and in my own life, if the writer's living is high quality and his thinking productive, the actual time he spends in the act of writing (alone, sitting down) is a small percentage of his life. And yet it is exactly this smaller part that makes him a writer, beyond merely living and talking.

Because the writer's "studio time" needs to be spent in living, I believe he develops more slowly than all other artists. More than a ballerina or a pianist, who may have started in childhood and developed excellent technique by the age of twenty, the writer may long ago have mastered grammar, vocabulary and penmanship, but what, at age twenty, does he or she have to say? Granted, there are exceptions. Some people live a lot of life early. But they are rare exceptions.

Add ten years of living to the twenty-year-old aspiring writer, and if he has taken risks, walked through open doors, launched out into uncharted seas, he surely has something of greater significance to write about at age thirty. Add ten more years to his life. After forty or forty-five years of living, the writer's view of life, his ideas, his thoughts are apt to be more seasoned, more sharply honed, of greater depth and simplicity. He is apt to know firsthand much more that is worth sharing with others.

But you, the youthful one reading this, do not take offence or become discouraged. No! If you have an inclination to write, do it. Set your hand and shoulder to the task. Do it. You will see if you love words enough—and people. You will see if it seems good to you also. And the more you write, the more you gain a facility to translate into words on paper, the greater will be your ease to say on paper the deeper insights and experiences you have lived.

The preceding discussion has all been to the general question of how to write. I have shared with you in detail Luke 1:1-4 and Acts 4:20. And then I have gone on to give you certain of my firsthand experiences in these areas of truth.

Before we go on to the why of writing, let me handle a question I have given much thought. It has come to me again and again from aspiring writers in our ministry.

The question: How does one handle conflict? How does a believing writer, who knows Christ is coming back and that all the problems of this life are temporary and insignificant compared to his return, how does he present and handle conflict (another word for conflict might be negatives)?

When I first heard Power for Abundant Living, I came to it from a world so overwhelmed by negatives that the sweet "God bless you" and "Isn't life wonderful" I heard were utterly and completely refreshing.

However, as I began learning to walk the walk, growing progressively aware of the mighty spiritual battle surrounding me and beginning to experience the hatefulness of the Adversary in numerous situations, I found the insipid droning of the "Isn't life grand" theme too superficial, not telling the whole story. Such a wispy attitude of "Everything is fine. Nothing ever goes wrong" annoyed me. I did not want to be a Pollyanna writer. Yes, I believed Christ is coming back. Yes, I was sure God had all matters firmly in hand. Yet, almost every day, I was confronted by details of negatives, by specifics of the spiritual battle.

So I had a conflict: How do I deal with conflict in writing? Life is not a simplistic string of goody-goods. I, myself, get bored reading much of such stuff. It does not tally with day-to-day reality as I know it. Yet I certainly did not want to go the way of the world: stating and restating the problems ad nauseum.

The truth is, we are in a spiritual battle. Conflict is a reality. Then, how do we handle it? It took some study and thinking on the question, but the answer is there in God's Word. Certainly negative situations—death, sickness, confusion—abound in the Word. How are they handled?

First of all, the sufferings of Christ are never mentioned without speaking of his glory also. Sufferings and glory always go together. So we can state the problem, bring up conflict, BUT always with the certainty that there is a solution and resolution. Although negatives come up in life, it would be dishonest for us as believing writers to set them down alone, as though we knew no answers. We know there are answers. Negatives come up. Conflict comes up. We can record it, BUT ALWAYS in the context of the solution, the answers. That is one thing we can offer that the world does not—indeed, cannot—offer.

I have seen in my own writing, and in the writings of others, that it is much easier to make the negatives juicy and alive than to make the positive situations lively. I attribute this to our years of conditioning by the world to relish the vivid negatives of life and to pass over lightly the good, the whole, the positive.

That shows me we need to study, to work the Word, read the Word, and get our thinking positively conditioned. The positive must be at least as easy to get excited about and to present as the negative. We are simply unpracticed at thinking God's way.

So in a piece of writing we may show conflict, but always in the greater context of answers, solutions and resolutions from the Word of God. Our goal as writers is to edify, to build up the reader, and so to build up the Body of Christ.

Conflict is, in fact, essential to much writing. It inspires interest, keeps the reader reading. The challenge is to present conflict accurately in the context of answers from God's Word. Conflict exists spiritually between darkness and light. As long as we are in the world, we are surrounded by darkness. Yet, at the same time, we are light. And so we see conflict between spiritual darkness and spiritual light.

I began this section by posing the question, "How do we as writers handle conflict?" This question made us aware of darkness—lack of spiritual understanding. I then brought in the Word—Christ's suffering always presented with Christ's glory. The Word brought in light. The light gave us our answer and resolved the conflict: we speak of problems with their solutions. We bring up questions (darkness) to show their answers so that:

> Ephesians 1:18 and 19:
> The eyes of your understanding being [can be] enlightened; that ye may know what is the hope of his calling, and what the riches of the glory of his inheritance in the saints,
> And what *is* the exceeding greatness of his power to usward who believe.

While the question was posed, darkness was revealed. Conflict prodded our minds. That conflict ("Good question—what's the answer?") inspired you to read further. You wanted the darkness melted. You wanted to see the light, the resolution.

Now, this has been an example of handling conflict in the essay form, a form dealing with the presentation of ideas (essay definition: the logical and systematic development of a series of ideas upon a given theme. In this case, our theme is stated in the title: *On Writing*). But conflict may be handled similarly in a poem, novel or an article form.

Some darkness, some negative is introduced, perhaps in the form of a question. Conflict is revealed. Perhaps between what is and what could be, or between one character, an unbeliever, and another character, a believer. Such conflict is true, often necessary, but as the reader reads, the eyes of *his* understanding must be opened, enlightened, so that the conflict, the darkness, is dispelled by the light.

Remember our discussion on the structure of a novel? The main character is faced with a problem—conflict. The Word of God sets forth this very pattern. God is faced with a problem. What will He do now? How will He handle it? How will the details unfold? Here is conflict. But remember also the conflict is totally resolved, and all the way through we are reminded of the answer, the promise—the coming of Jesus Christ and of this sufferings and glory.

To summarize this section on how to write from the Word of God, let us look at yet another "seminar on how to write." In Luke, all the questions on the what, how and why of writing were handled in four verses. In Habakkuk 2:2, we have the what, how and why in one verse:

> And the Lord answered me, and said, Write the vision, and make *it* plain upon tables, that he may run that readeth it.

Here, so simply stated in one short verse, we have the what, how and why of writing. In fact, it is the what, how and why of all forms of communication, of the arts and of moving God's Word.

"And the Lord answered me...." God is always giving us the answer. His Word answers all our questions in everything pertaining to life and godliness.

Now this verse is in the Old Testament. God is speaking to Habakkuk in a particular instance, regarding a specific vision. But we also know that Habakkuk was a holy man of God, who spoke as he was moved by the spirit of God upon him. And whatever God revealed to him in that particular vision cannot contradict anything that God has revealed in His written Word. God cannot contradict Himself.

God said: "Write the vision." Vision is what we receive when we learn what God has made available to us. Vision is what is available according to God's Word. As we study God's Word, we see what He has made available and the consequences of not availing ourselves of it.

What we write is vision—we let people know what is available from God. The same is true of any of the arts. The dancer dances what is available from God. The painter paints; the architect builds; the singer sings; the musician plays some aspect of WHAT IS AVAILABLE from God according to His Word. That is vision. All the arts are designed to communicate some truth of WHAT IS AVAILABLE from God—VISION.

How do we write? We "make *it* plain upon tables."

We write to be understood. We write simply, lay it out before our readers like a map. So, too, the how of the other arts. We dance, paint, sing, play, build, speak to be plainly understood so others can easily receive the vision of what is available from God.

And why do we write? "That he may run that readeth it!" We write plainly, clearly, simply, showing what is available so the reader will run the race with patience, so that he will run with God. Or, to put it negatively, so that the reader will flee, run *from* evil, avoid broken fellowship. That is why we write. We want to move our reader to move God's Word.

Put this verse side by side with Luke 1:1-4. Here, from the Word of God, is all the instruction a writer needs. Here is the way to write. The what, how and why of writing—God has given us vision and opened our understanding. Now, it is for us as writers, to run with that vision.

*   *   *

Previously, I touched on the life-style of the writer and the process of writing itself. I would like to expand upon that theme by approaching it from a very familiar, foundational verse of scripture. I have given much thought in my life to the whole question of "perspiration vs. inspiration" in writing. II Peter 1:21 opened my understanding in this area:

> For the prophecy came not in old time by the will of man: but holy men of God spake *as they were* moved by the Holy Ghost.

What a wonderful verse of scripture. When I first read and thought about it, I saw these holy men dramatically "moved." I saw their guts churn within them, saw them sit down with bold gestures and begin to write the Word of God. After all, they were inspired, right? Inspired by God, moved by the holy spirit upon them, right? Ah, to have such inspiration from God; ah, to let God do all the work and just turn my insides, giving me words in neat order, I thought. So, I waited around to be "moved" as my mind had initially pictured the process.

Such was my understanding of this verse. Then one day, with a deadline glaring at me from my calendar, having thrown away another and another and another meaningless false start on an article, my mind pathetically gray and blank, I remembered this verse.

Surely, as a believer with Christ in me, desiring to speak (or write, in this case) for God to God's people, I was like these "holy men who spake." Surely, if God could "move" them in those days, He could "move" me today. Why was nothing happening? Why was my mind dull as a desert? Why was I not inspired? Why did my guts not churn with something other than nervousness? Why was I not running to my desk with dramatic gestures to record words pouring out in ordered fashion through my mind?

As I scowled at these questions, I began to wonder what that word "moved" really meant. The more I thought about it, the more I realized I really had no idea. If I had no idea what it was to be "moved by the holy Ghost," how on earth could I then recognize God moving in me?

As if by inspiration, I cast aside pen, paper, article, forgot the blankness of my recalcitrant mind, and ran for my Bullinger's Concordance.

What was it to be "moved by the Holy Ghost"? This study so relieved and enlightened me that I desire to share this truth with you here. Yes, we are holy men and women today, filled with holy spirit. Yes, God works in us both to will and to do of His good pleasure.

The word "move" (*pherō*) means to "carry or bear." This is the only time it is translated "moved." Most often, it is rendered "bring" (33 times), "bear" (eight times), "bring forth (five times); twice it is rendered "endure," and it is translated "carry," "lay," "lead," "move," "reach," "reach hither," "up-hold" and "go on" one time each."

I stared in amazement at this information. Where were my churning insides that I had so vividly pictured? Where were the emphatic gestures? Nowhere in evidence at first glance. What then did *pherō* really mean? I desired to know it accurately.

According to Bullinger, *pherō* is "to bear or carry a load (with the idea of motion;) to bear as fruit, to endure, bear with." The word was rendered into Latin as *fero*, *fer* becoming the word for "iron," the strongest known metal that could carry or bear or endure. The word *fer* comes from Latin into current English usage as anything having to do with iron—as in ferrous metals, ferro electric, ferro concrete, ferro magnetic and numerous other terms. "Ferrous" refers to anything containing iron. Such is the development of the word *pherō* in the last two thousand years. But what were the connotations? What is its meaning here in II Peter?

And so, I proceeded to look up every usage of the word—and to write down each verse where it appeared twinkling like a precious gem, beckoning me to plumb the depths of its very meaning.

I shall not render the complete study here. You may do that for yourself if your own curiosity is piqued sufficiently. But to give you some insight, let me share one passage where this word *pherō* glitters in profusion. Jesus Christ is speaking to his disciples (his words are spirit and they are life):

John 15:1-8:
I AM the true vine, and my Father is the husbandman. Every branch in me that beareth (*pherō*) not fruit he taketh away: and every *branch* that beareth (*pherō*) fruit, he purgeth it, that it may bring forth (*pherō*) more fruit.
Now ye are clean through the word which I have spoken unto you.
Abide in me, and I in you. As the branch cannot bear (*pherō*) fruit of itself, except it abide in the vine; no more can ye, except ye abide in me.
I am the vine, ye *are* the branches: He that abideth in me, and I in him, the same bringeth forth (*pherō*) much fruit: for without me ye can do nothing.
If a man abide not in me, he is cast forth as a branch, and is withered; and men gather them, and cast *them* into the fire, and they are burned.
If ye abide in me, and my words abide in you, ye shall ask what ye will, and it shall be done unto you.
Herein is my Father glorified, that ye bear (*pherō*) much fruit; so shall ye be my disciples.

In this passage the context of the word *pherō* is the bearing of fruit. Now, there is a condition to this bearing of fruit, which is the other Greek word so often used in this passage: *menō*, here translated *abide*—meaning to remain, to stay, to rest. This is the one condition of *pherō*, bearing fruit.

In order to *pherō* (bear fruit), we must *menō* (abide, stay, remain on the vine, Jesus Christ). In verse 5: "He that abideth (*menō*) in me, and I in him, the same bringeth forth (*pherō*) much fruit." And in verse 8: "Herein is my Father glorified, that ye bear (*pherō*) much fruit."

God wants us to *pherō*—to bear fruit. For when we bear fruit, we glorify Him. The only way we can bear fruit is to abide. That is the condition. Shall we abide in Him, and let His words abide in us? If we abide, remain, stay faithful to His Word, WE CANNOT HELP BUT bear fruit (*pherō*).

How much groaning do you hear from the apple trees outside in early summer? How much travail, how much effort do they show in bringing forth their fruit? Why, none at all. The apple tree bearing apples just grows. The fruit simply appears in due season. No strain. No sweat. No groanings. If the tree is alive and it happens to be a fruit tree, the fruit simply comes.

Here then is the proper connotation of *pherō*. Yes, holy men of God spake. They spake. They wrote down the Word, as they *were moved* (*pherō*) by the holy ghost. The Holy Spirit raised them up. God carried them. God bore them up. God held them up. Now, in order for God through His holy spirit to have done that, they must have *abided* in Him, remained, stayed faithful, rested in Him. And as they abided, He raised them up to the due season, when the fruit simply came. In this case, II Peter 1:21, the fruit was the prophecy, the written prophecy, the Word of God we read today.

How clearly we can see this in the lives of God's men

throughout the Word of God. Take Moses, for example. Did not God have His hand upon Moses in Egypt, when as a newborn baby he floated down the Nile in a reed basket, where he was found by Pharoah's daughter and then raised in Pharoah's court as a son? Did not God have His hand upon Moses after he had killed an Egyptian and fled into the wilderness, finding his way to the Midianite camp? Did not God have His hand upon Moses when he tended sheep, married, had two sons, first climbed Mount Horeb, when he stopped to investigate the burning bush? Did not God then speak to Moses directly, lead him, raise him, carry him, guide him, bear him up through His holy spirit upon him, so he could return to Egypt, confront Pharoah and lead the children of Israel out of Egypt? Did not God have His hand upon Moses through forty years in the wilderness, through a cloud by day and a pillar of fire by night, through talking to him face to face and mouth to mouth?

Was not this man born, carried, raised up by the holy spirit to that place where in due season he sat down and wrote the Word of God? And that writing must have come as apples on the tree in midsummer. But all along, throughout his life, he was moved (*pherō*) by the holy ghost, and the fruit, the writing, was a "natural" outcome of the holy spirit carrying him, bearing him up.

Because the Word says so in II Peter 1:21, this must be how God worked with all His holy men who spake—wrote the Word—for Him. He brought them up, carried them by His holy spirit, and they produced the fruit—writing—in due season. These men must have been abiding in Him, must have stayed their minds on Him.

And this is our great key also as writers in this administration. Our responsibility is to abide in Him and to let His Word abide in us—then He shall raise us up also, carry us up to where the writing comes as a natural result of our living and thinking with Him. So let us abide in Him, and let Him raise us up.

This word study on that wearisome day enlightened my understanding. I had then to restructure my thoughts to agree with truth. Out went the churning insides, the lightning bolts, the dramatic gestures, for I saw that God did not move in His holy men in that way. And neither would He move in me in that way.

My responsibility was simply to abide in God. He had carried me this far, even all those years when I had not known Him. He had put in my heart a desire to write, had opened doors for me to develop through assignments, through publication. And He had carried me to this place also where I had a responsibility and a deadline (which He knew, too) to write an article. Would He desert me here? No, He cannot desert us. He is faithful. And so, the ideas would have to appear, sparkling, dancing like the fruit on heavily laden boughs in the warmth of glowing summer.

And guess what happened? I relaxed. I stopped trying to work my way to glory. I set my priorities straight: I simply abode in Him. I began again. An idea appeared in my mind, a simpler way to organize. And then another idea, another thought, so obvious I wondered why I had not seen that before. Yes, that was good right here, and the words followed meekly one after another in simple sentences, paragraphs, sections and it was done. I liked it. It was good—simple, straight, edifying.

I have shared this incident and some of my mental struggles because I believe it will help you. Not just the rearranging of priorities, putting God first in everything,, but because the most significant exhortation of this incident is our constant, continuous, crying need to go to God's Word to set our thinking straight and to receive our inspiration for doing anything. Our works (writing, the other arts, anything) need to spring directly, naturally, as it were, from our life with God, our fellowship with Him. Let us abide (*menō*) in Him and let His words abide in us. Then we also shall be moved (*pherō*), brought up, carried, borne by Him to produce fruit in due season.

Let us now consider more closely the question of why we write. I have already given answers from the Word of God regarding what our writing does for others.

Luke 1:4:
That thou mightest know the certainty of those things, wherein thou hast been instructed.
Habakkuk 2:2:
. . . that he may run that readeth it.

I am as altruistic as anyone else. But I know from God's Word He wants me to profit, to benefit. He wants His writers to be blessed, delivered, fulfilled and made whole, so that they can pass on His goodness from an overflow of heart in the love of God. I would therefore like to examine more closely the benefits to you, the writer.

I have said previously that writing in itself is a

renewed-mind tool. I shall show you this in the Word of God. But first, set in your mind how available and accessible writing is to you. If you are reading this, you are literate. You are already physically able to write. Probably you are already writing a certain amount in your daily life without giving the matter much thought. You may dash off letters, notes, lists of groceries to buy, lists of things to remember, things to do. Perhaps you keep a journal or diary of sorts. Perhaps you make notes at teachings. In any case, I am pointing out that the medium of writing is probably already a part of your life.

The tools needed are also very accessible and available: pen (or pencil) and paper. You do not need a typewriter, although if you have one you can use that, too. But the basics—pen and paper—are easily available, easily replaceable, inexpensive, do not require expert repairmen or hard-to-find spare parts.

The third necessary element is also at hand. Pen and paper do not leap into motion by themselves. They need you, but you do not need anything else to write. You are your material. The things you set to paper are from you—your thoughts, your ideas, your impressions, your observations, your way of seeing things. These you carry with you always. No chance to leave them behind.

This may sound simple, but I want you to see how available, how close writing is to you. You are doing it already. There is nothing to order by mail for which you must wait.

There is a built-in quality in the act of writing itself. Writing forces the mind to concentrate on one thing at a time. Writing necessitates linear thinking. Words can only be set down on paper one at a time. Writing slows down the mind so it can concentrate on one word at a time. And the very act of writing itself engages the whole mind.

Our minds operate at a fantastic speed. Thoughts, images, phrases, feelings, run through our minds at a phenomenal rate. We think at a rate of 850-1,000 words per minute. But we speak only at a rate of 100-125 words per minute. Thoughts flow faster than spoken words. Also, spoken words flow faster than written words can be set down. So the act of writing slows the mind and causes intense concentration on one word at a time in some logical sequence. Can you see why writing is a spectacular renewed-mind tool to build concentration, to develop the stayed mind? (No wonder we were encouraged in The Way Corps to write down goals, write down schedules, write a diary, write down ideas, write, write, write.)

Also, once written down, our words (thoughts) are no longer vague and elusive. Once written, the words can be read, reconsidered, examined. Are they logical? Are they worthwhile? Do they make sense? Are they profitable?

Not so with our thoughts or spoken words—unless we deliberately plan to remember or record them. Once thought, they are apt to melt, reappearing later in some other context. Once spoken, our words have evaporated into thin air. Were they logical? profitable? worthwhile? Did they make sense? It's hard to say. There is nothing to put your finger on. But written words stare back at you with a smirk or a challenge or a smile. They can be reconsidered in detail.

All right, the tools of writing are at hand. Yes, writing down words offers considerable mental control. Yes, we are using the medium already. But now, why do it any more than we are already? Why write?

The very first usage of the Hebrew word transliterated *kathab*, meaning "to write, inscribe or describe," is in Exodus 17:14a:

> And the Lord said unto Moses, Write this *for* a memorial in a book, and rehearse *it* in the ears of Joshua.

Notice, God commanded Moses to write His words in a book for a memorial— that these words would be in black and white before the people (not just thoughts and spoken words). He wrote the words so they could be referred to again and again, tangibly. And then God tells Moses to rehearse—to speak—these same words in the ears of Joshua.

God did not say: Write this in a book and give the book to Joshua to read. No, Moses was to write the words for a benefit to his own renewed-mind walk, because writing down God's Word himself would provide the benefit of cementing these words in his own mind!

I am so excited about the greatness of this single truth; let me show it to you again in more detail. In Deuteronomy 17:14-20, God is talking to Moses, laying down the Law. Right here, God is not only forthtelling, but also He is foretelling what will transpire with Israel at a future date, once they have come into the Promised Land. He is foretelling of Saul, David, Solomon and more.

Deuteronomy 17:14-17:

When thou art come unto the land which the Lord thy God giveth thee, and shalt possess it, and shalt dwell therein, and shalt say, I will set a king over me, like as all the nations that *are* about me;

Thou shalt in any wise set *him* king over thee, whom the Lord thy God shall choose: *one* from among thy brethren shalt thou set king over thee: thou mayest not set a stranger over thee, which *is* not thy brother.

But he shall not multiply horses to himself, nor cause the people to return to Egypt, to the end that he should multiply horses: forasmuch as the Lord hath said unto you, Ye shall henceforth return no more that way.

Neither shall he multiply wives to himself, that his heart turn not away: neither shall he greatly multiply to himself silver and gold.

God is foretelling of the time the children of Israel shall demand a king, and God has laid out the things this king should not do. Now, here is the big verse; here is what this king should do.

Deuteronomy 17:18 and 19:

And it shall be, when he sitteth upon the throne of his kingdom, that he shall write him a copy of this law in a book out of *that which is* before the priests the Levites:

And it shall be with him, and he shall read therein all the days of his life: that he may learn to fear the Lord his God, to keep all the words of this law and these statutes, to do them.

Look at this! Why should this king write himself a copy of the Law? He has the priests, the Levites, some of whom were scribes, whose job it was to copy the Scriptures. The king need not write a copy of the Law because no one else can write, for others could write. Why then should the king write himself a copy of this

Law in a book? There must be a benefit—a great benefit to himself personally.

Look at the benefit: "And it shall be with him." After he writes it, the Word shall be with him. The more effort put forth, the more received and retained. It is a matter of principle. If the king writes his own copy, it will be with him deeper, longer. He still must read (and reread) God's Word—"and he shall read therein all the days of his life." But look further at the benefits of writing first, then reading and rereading: "that he may learn to fear the Lord..." and "to keep all the words of this law..." and "to do them." Here are more benefits.

> Deuteronomy 17:20:
> That his heart be not lifted up above his brethren, and that he turn not aside from the commandment, *to* the right hand, or *to* the left: to the end that he may prolong *his* days in his kingdom, he, and his children, in the midst of Israel.

This tremendous truth from God's Word—the personal benefits of writing (writing God's Word being the most profitable) to develop stayed-mind discipline and mental concentration, both necessary to success—did not go unnoticed by the world either.

Again and again the great men of history, the great achievers—who were not thought of as writers—wrote. What schoolboy or girl who has had the privilege of studying Latin does not know the opening lines of Julius Caesar's *The Conquests of Gaul*: "All Gaul is divided into three parts...." Yet, we do not think of Julius Caesar as a writer. He was an emperor, a general, a leader of men. He was a statesman, a politician (he must have been busy!) and, yet, he wrote, and his words are read today. Surely, he recognized a benefit to himself to make time to do this.

Our own John Adams kept a journal for thirty years, from his days at Harvard until his second ambassadorship to Europe. We know him also as a statesman, a politician, a leader, but he made time to write, and wrote faithfully—for himself.

Michelangelo we think of as a sculptor, an architect, a great painter, but he set down his innermost conflicts and prayers to God in poetry, in sonnets. These can be read today. Leonardo da Vinci—inventor, painter, scientist, mathematician, military engineer—kept voluminous notes (in mirror writing) on all his observations and inventions. Beethoven, whom we know as a composer and musician, kept journals, notes. Van Gogh, the painter, was a prolific writer of letters. These are but a few examples.

We think of none of these men as writers at all. They are recognized producers of major works still extant today, works far superior to those of many of their peers. Their production required tremendous stayed-mind concentration, great mental discipline, well-developed minds and imaginations. And all these men made time to write. Writing must have benefited them in their lives' endeavors.

Anywhere we see men of the world succeed on a small or grand scale, we know it is because they must be applying principles from the Word of God. So these men wrote, and we have seen how God encouraged his men to write—as well as read—His Word.

The act of writing is itself beneficial to the person

writing. A matter of principle, writing requires more concentrated mental effort put forth and, therefore, more may be received and retained.

Suffice it to conclude that God treasures a written word and that God raised up writers to hold forth His Word in this form also. Because of the potential outreach inherent in a written word, it can reach the most people in time and across space. And God is definitely interested in reaching people.

Isaiah 30:8:
Now go, write it before them in a table, and note it in a book, that it may be for the time to come for ever and ever.

Writing brings with it great satisfaction and great responsibility, for written words are powerful. People believe them because they are written.

There is so much more of interest in the field of writing—areas I have not so much as mentioned—style, figures of speech, verbs, nouns, structure, imagery, setting, characterization, poetry—ah, and so much more. The Word contains so much teaching in the area of writing. It shows even how to interview a person. There is so much I have not covered here and so much more I have not yet learned from the Word of God and life.

But I believe that in this essay, "On Writing," I have shared with you a basic foundation from the Word of God that will help you begin or continue writing with more direction and encouragement.

By God's mercy and grace, seeds have been planted. He shall have to give the increase and raise up His writers for our day and time. I rejoice to hear of anyone setting foot on the road to become a Christian writer, writing to move God's Word.

*   *   *

There are moments before a blank page when I become impatient, frustrated and want to cry out the immortal words of another writer (I guess) in a moment of frustration. In Job 19:23, Job cries out:

Oh that my words were now written!
Oh that they were printed in a book!

But such moments are far outweighed by the sweetness to the soul that accomplishment in this area brings the doer.

I carry with me three pictures of writing. And in my lost moments of anguish, I gently pull these pictures out and consider them once again. They never fail to refresh my soul. I would like to share these pictures with you, believing you may find in them some refreshment and inspiration also.

For me, writing is like being a jeweler. Every one of us is given at birth a leather pouch of most precious gems. Some, when they grow up, cast them before swine. Some never realize they have them in their possession. Some trade them for bread crumbs. The satchel of precious gems is our words, our words that we possess. The writer is the one who understands the immense value of these jewels. He treasures them.

Laying before himself a rich, velvet cloth of midnight blue, he opens his satchel and scatters its contents upon the cloth. He then picks up one, studies it, appreciates it, considers it. He then picks another and another—diamonds and sapphires and emeralds and jade and pearls and rubies. They sparkle before him, and the writer sets them into a necklace. He can give it away or wear it, but wherever that necklace goes, it brings with it beauty, sparkle, brilliance to the holder, as well-chosen words will always enrich and beautify both the speaker and the listener, the writer and the reader.

Writing is like skiing. If you have never skied, picture yourself on a cold, fresh winter morning, the first one up the chair lift. The air is clean and light as you ascend the mountain. The late morning sun sparkles diamonds on the snow everywhere below you, and in the beauty of the clear atmosphere, you have very soon attained the top of the mountain.

You glide to the edge of the slope. Before you lies a vast expanse of white, virgin snow. The first one there, you are free to choose how you will descend. You could go straight down, or tack right to left, or left to right. You can make broad or narrow diagonals.

In the fresh mountain air, in the crisp clarity of morning, you are free, free to go any way you choose. You know you will go from the top of this white expanse to the bottom, and in descending you will leave behind your pattern of tracks.

The white expanse is a blank sheet of paper. The writer stares at it, like a skier on the height of the slope, and he is free, free to fill it any way he chooses. He knows he will go from top to bottom and cover it with his own marks, his original pattern of tracks.

Writing is like handing a precious friend a cup of freshly squeezed juice. What, after all, do we have to share with one another but the fruit of the spirit in our lives? What can we give freely to one another but the love, joy, peace, gentleness, goodness, longsuffering, faith (believing), meekness and temperance that we have realized ourselves?

And so, our fellowship with one another as believers is the exchanging of the fruit of the spirit in our own lives. I see this "fruit of the spirit" as a bunch of plump, delicious grapes. As we fellowship together, we are constantly offering one another this refreshing fruit. Our fellowship with one another is sweet, like eating ripe grapes.

But the writer—the writer goes a step further. Clasping his hands together around his grapes, he squeezes them, squeezing from them fresh juice into a simple cup. The juice contains the best of the fruit, the most nutritious, the most easily ingested, the most digestible part. And the writer hands that cup of the very finest essence of the fruit of the spirit in his life to you, the reader.

Drink. Be refreshed. The writer's written words are the best of his life the writer has to offer. Let these words be sweet in the reader's mouth. Let them be satisfying. Let them linger pleasantly in the reader's mind—that he that readeth it may run—run even further and faster with God.

Essay Four

Thinking Through Forms

We who believe God and are born again in this Administration of Grace contain within our earthen vessels (our body/soul lives) a power most precious and rare—the same power that raised Jesus Christ from the dead after three days and three nights. Truly, the gift of God in us is of such an overwhelming magnitude that when we consider it honestly, we can only stand back in amazement and awe. This gift is a treasure; it is the greatest content ever known.

However, in this essay I am vitally concerned not with content, but with form. Why? For the simple reason that the communicability of the content is only as great as the greatness of the form that communicates it. (For a basic discussion on form and content, expression and communication, let me refer you to Essay Three, "Thinking through Words" in Part One of this volume.)

I am vitally concerned with form because so is God. His Word is our standard. Not only is the *what* (content) of God's Word magnificent and powerful, but also the *how* (form) of God's Word is equally magnificent and powerful. This is, in fact, our ministry. We investigate at close hand the perfection of the form of God's Word. We study the minute accuracy and integrity of God's Word, and, the more we see how perfectly, how beautifully each word fits together, the more we believe the content, the message of what God says. God's *how* of saying His message is as great as *what* He is presenting. The what and the how, the truth and the beauty, the content and the form of God's Word are integrated on an equally magnificent, perfect level. That is our standard, the state to which we also can aspire in our efforts.

Let me approach form from another direction. In an early session of the Power for Abundant Living class, Dr. Wierwille discusses "what to do with it when you have got it" (the third thing one must know in order to receive anything from God). He uses an illustration. Pointing to a pen on his desk, Dr. Wierwille says we learn from a very early age to receive things in the natural realm. "This is a pen. It is available." Then, he simply reaches out and takes it. He says: "Now, what do I do with it when I've got it? I can take this pen and use it as a toothpick. But," he continues, "that is not what it was designed for. The pen was designed for writing. The pen is best utilized for writing."

Forms can be misused. But we utilize them best in the function for which they were designed. If we needed to ride somewhere, we could ride a cow—and maybe even get there. But a cow is not best suited for riding. A horse would serve the purpose far better. God is concerned with form as well as content He is concerned with the best utilization. Look at His creation, the plant and animal kingdoms. Everywhere, God has provided the best utilization. Animals eat plants. When animals die, insects are equipped for garbage detail. Trees give off oxygen. Animals and man utilize oxygen and give off carbon dioxide that plants need. At every point of His creation, God has been minutely concerned with the smallest details of His forms in plants, animals and man. Insects do not have extra legs or unnecessary eyes. The fish which were designed for the depths of the ocean where it is dark have no eyes at all. God did not design the forms of His creation haphazardly. No, He designed everything with purpose—for the best utilization in a certain way.

I have already mentioned the form of the words in God's Word, put together in minutely detailed perfection. Nowhere in God's Word or in God's creation does He slough off in details of forms.

In Ephesians 5:1, the Word exhorts us, who are the faithful in service of Jesus Christ in the Administration of Grace, to be "followers of God," imitators of God, as dear children. If God has been and still is vitally concerned with the minute details of His forms, should we not also then be concerned about the forms of those things we make and do?

It is our responsibility as artists to be vitally concerned with the forms of what we produce. Hence, also the title of this essay: "Thinking through Forms."

I am concentrating particularly on forms in what we call the fine arts. As God designed everything in His creation for a best utilization, we, desiring to be imitators of Him, need to pay heed to the forms we use in the arts. Since forms can be misused, I am vitally concerned that we think through forms and employ them for their best utilization.

Everything man does and makes in the senses realm (services and goods) forms the culture in which he lives. Man's goods and services can be divided roughly into two categories: those activities that provide for the body, the physical man, and those that provide for his soul. To provide for the physical man we have such areas of human activity as agriculture, industry, business, government. To feed (or please) man's soul, we have the second general category of the fine arts—visual arts, music, literature, drama, dance, architecture, etc.

There is some overlap. We must have basic shelter. A hovel or a cave might do, but a palace or a ranch home, these please the soul. So architecture overlaps from survival arts to fine arts. In the same way we must have covering, clothing. But once we are warm and dry, we desire our clothes to have color, style, variety. This feeds the soul life of man. Thus clothing, or fashion design, enters the category of the fine arts.

Man cannot exist without basic food, tools, peace and order, basic shelter, basic clothing. He must provide for these needs. But these are not enough, for after the basics are taken care of, man longs after beauty, the "higher" qualities of life. And so, we have the fine arts. Although not in the physical survival category, the arts nevertheless meet equally vital soul needs of man. He may exist physically, but man does not really live unless his soul is also satisfied—his eyes, his ears, his mouth and nose, his touch and feelings.

I am in no way suggesting survival arts to be less important than the fine arts, as the body is not less important than the soul or the spirit that dwells therein. Man is a three-part being; all three parts are vital. However, in this discussion, we are concentrating on the fine arts—thinking through forms in the fine arts field.

The arts were all originally designed to communicate, to move God's Word. First, to lead someone to being born again, and then to help and continue aiding God's people to renew their minds to the greatness of God's Word. In the first stage—to lead someone to the new birth—WORDS ARE IMPERATIVE. There are only two kinds of words—spoken and written. A person cannot be born again without believing certain truths communicated in words.

But, once a person has heard these words and obeyed, once a person has put on in his mind the basics of Christ, once he is walking by the spirit (even though we all stumble now and then), he hungers more and more to experience through his five senses the greatness of what is available from God. He does not want to settle for less than the best in all his surroundings.

Hebrews 5:13 and 14:

For every one that useth milk *is* unskilful in the word of righteousness: for he is a babe.

But strong meat belongeth to them that are of full age, *even* those who by reason of use have their senses exercised to discern both good and evil.

When our senses have been exercised to discern both good and evil, our senses long to see that "good" at every hand. We long to see, hear, touch, feel, taste and smell the "good."

The arts enter the mind through the senses, appealing to one dominant sense (depending on the art) and then involving the other senses only secondarily.

Music, for example, enters the mind primarily through hearing, and through vibration it causes feelings of one kind or another. Music does little to stimulate taste, smell or sight unless the listener pushes his own mind "to see" certain appropriate pictures.

Dance enters the mind through seeing and involves strong kinetic (feeling), stimulation through sight. Dance is most often accompanied by music which enters the ear and also inspires feelings.

Architecture is primarily visual and kinetic. Architecture defines space and causes us "to feel" a certain way about ourselves and the people around us. But there is not much to be heard, smelled or tasted in architecture.

Painting, photography, drawing—these appeal primarily to the eye. The other four senses are only weakly stimulated, although a person of well-developed imagination and concentration may look intently at a landscape and smell the pines, hear the birds sing, feel the freshness of the morning air. But primarily, the entrance into the mind is visual in these forms.

In drama, we have a strong visual and kinetic appeal, like dance, but because drama is made up of people speaking words, we have the potential total involvement that words—and literature—bring. Words can bring in all the senses in equal force.

Literature—words—are heard or seen, but their very nature (they are symbols) gives them the greatest potential influence upon the whole mind, since all the senses can be equally involved through words.

Every art, every form, can potentially aid the viewer in renewing his mind to the greatness of God's Word.

Indeed, let me repeat, every art form was designed to do just that. The challenge to our artists is to utilize the form fully to bless and edify God's people the most. Each form of the arts has a place, a time, a purpose to do the most for God's people. So we who are artists need to think through form—particularly in the area of art in which we are involved—and then maximize the utilization of the form, using it for all it's worth, but not misusing it.

How do the arts relate? How do they reach people? What is the best vehicle (form) to emphasize this message in a particular situation? These are profitable questions for our artists to think through in detail. God will let us know what we cannot know by our five senses, but so much of this knowledge is available through study and research in the senses realm. We need to learn all we can.

I am not so knowledgeable in every area of art (from the point of view of a producer) that I can think through all the forms. Skilled craftsmen in each area will need to think these things through for themselves. But in certain areas of the arts, I do have adequate knowledge to present a broad structure which may suggest ideas and directions to you. Let me share one such area here.

Music is a form of art. The musical arts are all those which employ melody. Within the form of music, there are many, many varieties of forms. We can divide music into instrumental and vocal, and these can be combined in a variety of ways. A solo guitar is quite different from a solo flute. Each one has its quality, its potential for moving God's Word, for aiding in the renewed mind (for we know that no one can be born again from an instrumental solo). But once a person is born again, music (in the proper context of time, situation and need) can do much to aid and inspire the mind back into the presence of God.

Almost any instrument can be played solo, and then they can be combined—two flutes, two violins, two pianos—or two different ones—violin and piano, flute and harp. So we can have instrumental duets (two instruments), trios (three), quartets, quintets, sextets, octets and on up to a full orchestra of 120 musicians all playing a variety of instruments in all types of musical forms.

I am not just trying to make a list of combinations here. All these combinations have a different potential quality for moving the Word of God. It is up to our musicians and composers to know their tools, all their possibilities, to make the best choice in any given instance.

This is to speak broadly of instrumental music only. Then there is vocal music. Remember, these all are forms in music—but how different! What varied potential! What varied results!

Let us glance at the vocal side. We could have an unaccompanied soloist (male or female, of different voice qualities—soprano, alto, tenor, bass). Then we can have that one voice accompanied by a variety of instruments.

Each combination will produce a different quality. Put two voices together, or a group, a trio, quartet, quintet, sextet. Each combination has possibilities within itself of producing a very different effect. Keep adding voices and we arrive at great choruses, with or without soloists, with or without instrumental accompaniment.

After we have introduced the vocal into music, however, we have introduced words, and then the content of the words sung becomes of vital importance. The content and the form need to be appropriate.

Enter words, and we must pay careful attention to the content. Each form, each combination of voices and instruments can have the greatest total impact on the listener in a specific way. This is exactly what needs to be thought through in minute detail. Let me give you some examples, some food for thought.

The soloist in the spotlight on stage represents me, the listener. I identify with him. Now, one aspect of each of our walks with God is that we each have an intimate and personal, solo relationship (fellowship) with God, our Father. Should not the subject matter of the soloist be some aspect of that individual, intimate fellowship we each have with Him?

Or put a duet out front. We all have one-on-one relationships in the family. Two conveys best such themes as marriage, witnessing, undershepherding, friendship.

Put three on stage. Why, that's family. We are all part of a spiritual family. That is another context of our fellowship with God. Let it be a small group, like Joyful Noise, with instrumental accompaniment. Do you recognize them? They are your Twig, my Twig. On stage before our very eyes they play out various themes in the family: like-mindedness, harmony, helping one another, mutual support. What more appropriate theme for them to handle as a small group than themes of family—like-mindedness and Twig fellowship?

Now, let us run ahead. Is God not grand? Is He not majestic? All-powerful? All-knowing? Is He not glorious beyond the imagination? These are qualities of God of which we need reminding and before which we stand in awe.

Bring on the chorus—a hundred voices. Bring on the soloists, trained to sing into the ears of thousands without amplification. Ah, the beauty of the human voice, the voice that God gave. What a versatile, magnificent instrument to make known His Word! Back up our chorus, our soloists, with a full orchestra including tympani and basses. Let them all together sing praise to God, to His glory, His magnificence. Would such a form not do justice to the greatness and grandeur of such a theme?

I believe it would be a misuse of form for the soloist to undertake this theme, as it would be for such a grand chorus to try to convey some aspect of our most intimate, personal and individual fellowship with Him. Sure, the Word may be sung—but we are concerned here with the best utilization of forms, forms, forms, designed for a specific purpose in moving God's Word. I am equally certain that we do not commit gross errors in this area. We would not even consider bringing our 100-man chorus to the evening Twig. We laugh at the obvious stupidity of such an idea. But we are apt to err on the finer details. Let us not use the pen to pick our teeth, but to write—thinking through forms.

*   *   *

Let us look more closely, at the grand forms in

music—a fully trained chorus, soloists and full orchestra. Both opera (including operetta, musical comedy, musicals, etc.) and oratorio have, in form, the exact same elements. What then is the difference? Opera has a plot. In oratorio, there is no plot; the performers sing directly to the audience, with no pretense of presenting a human situation. In oratorio, no plot intervenes.

Therefore, to move the Word we desire the appropriate form with the appropriate material. Opera needs plot; therefore, this form is designed for communicating material from the Old Testament, the Gospels and the Book of Acts. Oratorio is direct. It is the proper form for the material of the Church Epistles, where the person emphasized is "we" and "ye"—the Body of Christ. Picture such a combination before an audience of 10,000, singing not a "hallelujah" chorus, but a "Christ in you" chorus—with direct eye contact between singer and hearer. What an impact!

And here is where forms have been misused in the past. Handel's *Messiah*, Bach's *St. Mattias Passion*, these are great musical works, magnificent oratorios. I cry when I hear them. The beauty of the music is moving, and they are scriptural. BUT, the form of oratorio was used to convey Old Testament and Gospel material. They did fine with what they did, but what greater impact they could have had, having handled the material of the Church Epistles in oratorio form.

Other great oratorios—and they are great musically—Mozart's *C Minor Mass*, K. 427, Beethoven's *Missa Solemnis*, Verdi's *Monzoni Requiem*—these all handle words of the Latin mass.

Musically, they are magnificent works. But how they could have driven home the Word with impact had they handled the "we" and "ye" of the Church Epistles in oratorio form.

Both opera and oratorio are grand musical forms. They have much in common with drama, especially the opera form, where the action is played out on stage, dramatized. But, there is an important difference between straight drama and its musical counterparts.

Dramatic presentations or spectacles initiate a phenomenon that has been called "the willing suspension of disbelief." This means when we, the spectators, go to a play, we know it is not real. We have no doubt that the actors are acting, that they are not really mad at one another, not really dying. We, the audience, know the situation is not real, even as we see it unfold before our eyes.

Yet, let the lights dim. Let the curtain open, let the actors but speak their lines with conviction, and we fall under the spell of this phenomenon. Willingly we suspend our disbelief. Given a well-acted dramatic production, we forget the world outside, forget the actors are acting. We believe. We identify. We throw our hearts and souls into the presentation, becoming angry, sad or suddenly glad at a reversal of bad fortune. We become those people we are seeing for a time, going through their states of mind and emotions. The play is over. The lights come up, and, looking at one another, we smile and enter the real world once again to find our taxis and go home to pay the babysitter. But for a short period we willingly suspended our disbelief to enter as fully as we were able the world and feelings of the actors on stage.

Now, in straight drama, once we are into it, the identification can be so strong (depending on the theme) that we become threatened, defensive. Straight drama can be very close to real life. Sometimes too close for comfort. And so, in straight drama, if the theme is such—too personal, too threatening, too demanding on the emotions—the spectator may draw back and put up walls. This is why the themes for straight drama must be appropriate to the dramatic form, and not too personal, so as to cause the viewer to close out the whole message.

But enter music. Make a dramatic presentation musical and the total unreality of the situation allows a greater freedom of themes that can be handled in this form. Music acts like a shoehorn, slipping the message easily into the mind of the viewer without his becoming threatened and defensive. Music eases the willing suspension of disbelief for a wider variety of themes to be presented.

So, in opera (a drama or story set to music) there is greater freedom in the handling of theme. More scope, more breadth, more depth of emotion and variety of elements can be forged together and accepted (received) by an audience.

Another set of alternatives available in working with written or spoken words comes with decisions on point of view. First or second person is extremely direct: "I" is personal and intimate; "you" can be accusing—the pointing finger. Either point of view must be handled with care to produce the desired effect. Either of these points of view can result in the reader feeling threatened, defensive or uncomfortable, causing him to put up unseen barriers and not receive the message at all.

Third person, on the other hand, is distant, indirect and nonthreatening. This is the person of Jesus' parables. We can all safely hear about "him" and "her" and "them." They run by some distance away from us, like a movie. Because this point of view is so safe, it encourages the reader (listener) to become involved—if he wills. No pressure is brought to bear. He may identify with "him," "her" or "them," but if he wills not to be involved, the action remains a distant incident. Third person is the gentlest point of view, so characteristic of God's Word, showing us what is available and then allowing us complete freedom of will to decide whether to become involved or not.

In this light, straight drama is like "I" and "you," the first and second persons—very direct—while opera and other musical forms lend more distance and paradoxically allow more involvement and intimacy with the theme.

Let me restate that I am not judging one form or one particular point of view as superior to another. Each has its best use and application. I am encouraging detailed thinking to produce the fullness of the desired effect.

The form of opera, I believe, is the most challenging of all the arts, fusing as it does all the arts and the greatest number of people. Costumes and setting fill the visual sense; music and words, the auditory. The whole production is also dramatic—so we have all the arts utilized simultaneously—musical, literary, dramatic and visual, plus all the backstage work of presentation. All the arts are used, and a large number of people must sustain a high degree of like-mindedness to realize the production.

As opera developed, its great impact and potential were utilized in presenting themes of a highly tragic and melodramatic nature—themes of great emotional involvement, for this form could carry such themes. But, in this I see again the misuse of form, as the high degree of emotional involvement was all to no profit.

I believe opera is a magnificent form to move the Word—for all the reasons that it was misused. The form itself drives a message home with impact, engaging as it does all five senses. Opera is a form larger, grander than life. Almost too much—but we in the audience do not perceive it as too much because of the integration of all the art forms and because it is couched in music. The form fills fully all five senses and is easy to be entreated.

I believe certain themes of the Word could be communicated effectively through opera, themes that should not be handled in straight drama—themes involving high, poignant and noble feelings. Such an opera could inspire great emotional involvement to the point of moving people in the audience to hold forth the Word with greater commitment.

Before we consider forms other than musical, let me note that each instrument, each voice has particular qualities that are best suited to convey particular themes. These all can be thought through. For example, the soprano voice has a very pure sound and needs to speak doctrine. Her voice is light, fine and not colored by excess emotion. The contralto, on the other hand, is colored by warm, maternal qualities. This voice needs to sing words like:

I Thessalonians 2:7:

But we were gentle among you, even as a nurse cherisheth her children.

Such words sung by a soprano would not have the greatest possible impact.

The tenor has his particular quality of voice, and the basso—he speaks for God, as in Ephesians 5:1:

Be ye therefore followers of God, as dear children.

On the instrumental side, the form of concerto is a purely instrumental form where a solo instrument—be it violin, piano, harp or anything else—is highlighted with a full orchestra. At moments the orchestra plays exclusively. At other moments, the orchestra is silent and the solo instrument plays alone. At other moments, they play together—solo instrument and orchestra—but always, always in harmony, always building musically together the theme, the climax and resolution—always building in harmony together.

I listened to this form, searched my heart, and asked for light. What was this form conveying? What could this form best communicate of God's Word? And then I saw. Why, the solo instrument is like the member in particular, the individual believer, and perhaps even the one with a gift ministry. He is highlighted. He is out front. He demands attention, earns respect through excellence, all to the purpose of leading, guiding, teaching, building up the Body of Christ. And the orchestra represents the whole Body together, working together in harmony, like-mindedness, each member fulfilling his part.

The solo instrument states a theme. The orchestra picks it up and develops it. The solo instrument states a countertheme, a variation on the original theme (doctrine). The orchestra picks that up and develops it. They build it together. Music, especially instrumental music, inspires feelings, brings up deep emotion. And in the concerto form I see the potential of "hearing" the Body of Christ working together in harmony, led by the man of God, edifying itself in love.

I cannot vouch for the intentions of composers of the past. I am endeavoring to discover the best utilization of specific forms. In music, instruments and voices, in all possible combinations, have a best utilization in moving the Word of God.

In thinking through the minute details of the forms, all these things can be considered to produce musical works that bless God's people. In musical conservatories similar considerations are studied under such course titles as: "Theory of Music," "Harmony," "Counterpoint," "Instrumentalization," etc. Various aspects of music are isolated and studied out minutely to see how best to put them together—this is knowledge available in the world. BUT, it is not presented in light of the accuracy of God's Word. This is what we, as artists, composers and musicians in this ministry need to study out, meditate upon, speak in tongues about, and work—music in the light of God's Word. We need to know our musical tools (and there are many), but also we need to be spiritually mature in considering their use in light of the accuracy of God's Word, always seeking to edify God's people.

*　　　　*

The history of the world shows the rise and fall of civilization after civilization. One culture has produced forms of art which spoke *from* the people at that time and *to* the heart of the people in it.

In fifth century Greece, for example, during the Golden Age, it was drama and comedy and a little later, sculpture. In Elizabethan England (1600s), again drama dominated the culture of the time. Shakespeare rode this crest. The form of drama spoke from the heart of the people and to the heart of the people at that time. It crossed social and economic barriers. The poor and uneducated as well as the noble and rich thronged to the Globe Theatre, for they recognized an accurate form and spokesman. They recognized a true picture of themselves.

In other cultures at other times, music was the form that predominated (for example, seventeenth century Middle Europe); at other times painting dominated, as in the Italy of the Renaissance. During the rise of the Roman Empire it was architecture, which again dominated from the late Middle Ages to circa 1600 in Western Europe, where the Gothic cathedrals of the period still stand today. Thousands of simple people helped to build them, brick upon brick, their names lost forever to history. Even the major architects are largely unknown. But again, this particular art form dominated for a period and involved many people's lives, for they could contribute something and the form spoke for them. The form was from the heart of the people of the time and, speaking to the people, communicated something of value to them.

In other nations at other times, it was literature. In

Russia, in the nineteenth and twentieth centuries, it has been the poets and writers who spoke for and to the people. Even to this day, poetry readings are nearly comparable to our rock concerts, and people throng to hear the poet declaim his poems.

In comparison to many nations the world, America is young in development, and the first hundred years or more of this nation were spent in developing the physical phases of life—the survival arts. The land had to be claimed and subdued so that people could exist first. Only after that could the fine arts develop here.

What have been the dominant forms in our culture in the last two generations? I believe the more recent forms to emerge, forms that speak from and to a large segment of the American people, have been film (now partially eclipsed by television) and athletics. Athletics is an extension of drama and dance. It is spectacle and, like drama and dance, has the strongest kinetic appeal through sight and hearing. Also, the particular brand of music called rock and roll in the last generation, with its variations, has been a dominant form in our culture.

After all, what does the schoolboy or schoolgirl desire to grow up to be? A movie star, a star athlete perhaps or a rock star. Who wants to be a composer, a poet, a dancer or the president? Not many. The forms that have spoken from and to our people in America today have centered on the film industry, athletics and rock music. Notice that these forms are all highly physical and built on the individual. Who can replace Elizabeth Taylor? Babe Ruth? These forms are not as lasting and deep as some others—for example, literature.

As I observe the American cultural scene on the eve of the 1980s, it looks like these dominant forms are losing their hold. There is a distinct atmosphere of searching for perhaps deeper, more lasting forms that capture the aspirations, the dreams, the things of value in the life-style today. So it is a time of confusion, a good time to see some Word-centered forms arise in the culture. They will stand out in the general sea of vagueness and apathy with their simplicity, solidity and integrity.

*　　　*　　　*

Literature has not yet been the dominant form in American culture, even though we have produced several great writers in the past. As I have previously laid out some of the considerations in thinking through forms in music, so I would now like to make a few observations on form in literature.

In the previous essay, "On Writing," I indicated some of the major forms in the Word of God, discussing such forms as the novel, essay, journalism, biography, history, short story, screenplay, science fiction and poetry.

As the musician and composer desiring to move God's Word through their medium need to think through the details of musical forms to choose the best, so also the writers in our ministry today need to think through the tools of their medium—the written word— to choose the best form in which to present their themes.

Since I did not discuss poetry in detail previously, I should like to turn our attention to it here. Remember, in thinking through literary forms, we are endeavoring to discover: For what is the form best suited? How can

I get the best utilization of the form, and use it as it was designed, to move the Word of God most efficiently?

Poetry is a form of the written word, distinguished by its employment of a recognizable pattern, usually rhyme or rhythm. Thus, the poet sets himself an added limitation. He not only sets down an idea in words, but also he sets it down within a certain self-imposed pattern. It is the most economical of word forms, every word being absolutely noninterchangeable. Once a poem is set, there is no other way to set it.

But even though poetry is written down, it is primarily an oral form. A poem is to be read or recited aloud. Like drama, it is written down to pass on the particular combination of words accurately to other generations. But, as drama is written primarily to be played (although one can read it and enjoy it), so poetry is written to be declaimed, spoken before people.

In the mind, poetry has much in common with song. But because a song is carried by melody, the words (the ideas) need to be simpler and more repetitious. And how effective a song is in embedding itself in the mind, I am certain we have all experienced. Suddenly, walking down the street, driving in our cars, sitting at lunch, the phrase, the melody and words of a certain song spring unbidden into our minds, and we find ourselves humming and singing it over and over again. What a gentle aid to our renewed minds, if such a snatch of song should call us back to the Word of God from our daily preoccupations.

Both poetry and song have a strong mnemonic factor. Thus Alexander Solzhenytsin, a very prolific contemporary prose writer, in the Soviet forced-labor camps for eleven years wrote without pencil stub or paper, composing voluminous works in his mind in catchy rhyme patterns so that he could remember the material when he was released from prison. Poetry, like song, is more easily remembered.

Because a poem does not have melody, the idea or image it presents can be more involved, more complex, more thought-provoking. But in the same way as a song, a poem has the tendency to reappear in the mind, engaging one's thoughts to dwell upon the images inherent therein.

So the poet declaiming his poem before people accomplishes an effect very similar to the singer singing his song before an audience. If the song and singer are good, if the poem is beautiful and the poet bold and fearless, declaiming with conviction, we in the audience identify. That performer sets before our minds an indelible example, a powerful image. And in the audience, whether we be twelve people or twelve thousand, we sit and listen, actually thinking the same thing. We are for that time like-minded. Concentrating on the concept, the beauty of words, the boldness of the poet, we are actually living the like-mindedness the Word exhorts us to live. We are doing it!

Of course, the same result occurs when we sit before a teaching of the Word of God. As we all listen, we track on the same thoughts, we dwell in the same mental context. But there is room in a teaching situation to have a song, to have a poem, for the particular qualities of these forms do something else for people. They can help the people to relax, can set their minds toward a favorable direction, can help prepare their minds to receive the greatness of the teaching.

So poetry, the very individual manner of setting one's idea to words and sharing it with others, offers the one reciting a unique opportunity to give of himself and to give others the opportunity to be like-minded for the time being around the greatness of God's Word.

I see poets arising all over our country. After dinner, struck by an engaging idea that must have been inspired by the Christ within, the poet excuses himself, sets it down, works it over, is pleased, and by 7:30 p.m. when the Twig walks in for the evening fellowship, with a sparkle in his eye, he boldly, if a little breathlessly, recites his poem to the Twig. Ah, it is to the point. Ah, we understand. It is beautiful! Everyone listens, takes it in. As one mind, all who are present track the words of the poem in their thoughts, dwelling upon the delicate images, the inspiring suggestions. Everyone is blessed, pleased. For all have seen another example of the spirit of God moving in His people to bless, to inspire, to edify.

Perhaps someone who is listening at the time makes a decision. The next time some image or some idea strikes him, he will take the time, rather than sweeping it out of his mind, to sit down, to write it, to make it into a poem—the Word of God from his very own heart, worked in his own life, stated in his own vocabulary. He will see it through to the place of sharing with others a completed work (accomplishment is sweetness to the soul). And yes, at the next Twig meeting he gives in this manner. He recites his poem, and you know what? It is exactly on the theme the teacher is teaching tonight, though neither poet nor teacher even knew what the other was going to do!

So I have touched upon poetry. We would not normally get up in Twig and read from a novel. No, that form has a different place, purpose, design. Neither did I begin to set these ideas on paper in the form of a novel or a poem. No, I am sharing ideas here. I desire for the reader to follow them logically, systematically, without interference of a self-imposed rhythm or rhyme pattern which would draw attention away from the ideas. So this is an essay form. Now, I could have set these ideas in a novel, put thoughts into the mouths of characters, have them argue over various points. But that would still detract from the ideas, and my desire is that you have the best possible opportunity to follow through the material without hindrance.

Now, I had to be somewhat acquainted with my methods. I had to think through the forms of the written word available to me to make this decision. This is what I mean by thinking through forms. It is our joy and responsibility as artists, as producers and doers of the Word of God, to THINK, and while we are at it, to think through the forms.

*   *   *

As all the forms of music and literature have their best utilization, so it is in the other arts. Drawing, painting in oil or watercolor, graphics, charcoal, crayon, ink, pencil—each medium has its best use including the themes and handling for which it was designed. Even in photography, whether color or black and white, each has its own purposes. The visual arts include a myriad of various forms. I am not going to think them through here. I do not know enough as a producer in these fields. But I know it must be available to see them clearly, for it is a matter of principle. Life is a matter of principle and so is art. It is the responsibility of each of us who accept the challenge to move God's Word through the arts to think through the forms accurately according to the Word of God.

I would, however, like to make a few observations on architecture. My understanding in this area was greatly enlightened by reading *The Memoirs of Albert Speer* several years ago. Speer was Hitler's chief architect, exterior and interior, and stage designer. I was amazed at the detailed understanding that both Hitler and Speer had concerning the use of architecture.

If we live in a cave or a hovel, our physical needs may be met. We are talking about survival arts. But when we begin to design shelter to fill certain mental needs, to influence the soul in certain ways, we are in the area of the fine arts. I do not doubt that Hitler had spiritual help in perceiving the detailed possibilities; nevertheless, they were dealing in principle, and it is in isolating the principle that I am interested.

Remember, architecture defines space. The handling of the space around us causes us to feel certain ways, to perceive ourselves in certain ways. Because we are led to feel a certain way about ourselves, architecture also colors our relations with the people around us. Now, architecture can be overcome by the renewed mind. It cannot control us, unless we let it. Nevertheless, it helps to see how architecture works on our minds through our senses. As it can cause a negative self-image and sour relations, architecture can encourage a positive self-image and bring people together pleasantly.

The Reichschancellory was one building Speer designed and built for Hitler. This was his official office as head of state. The architectural thinking behind it is thoroughly recounted in Speer's book. Deliberately, the building was designed long—à la railroad stations—and in the flavor of the Third Reich Nazi style somewhere between Pharoah's pyramids and a Cecil B. DeMille movie set. From the outside, the quality was monolithic—strong, solid, serious. Simple decoration, militaristic and heroic (eagles, swastikas, other symbols of the empire), did not detract from the monolithic stability of the overall form.

But the floor plan was a stroke of brilliance. Railroad style, the entrant walked into a reception room at one end, and to reach Hitler's office at the very opposite end, had to walk through one sumptuous drawing room into another, even more sumptuous, and through another even more so, on and on, each one more rich, more luxurious, for nearly one-half mile! This was the architectural introduction through which the visiting potentate had to pass to come into Hitler's office, which itself was comparatively simple and unassuming. This also was deliberate, to lend the leader a Spartan, self-sacrificing air. And so the layout was deliberately designed to exhaust and intimidate Hitler's visitors. By the time they had arrived to face him across his impressive desk, they were ready to agree; they were in awe, confident of his power. Thus the architecture in this instance deliberately defined Hitler's inaccessability, power, heroism and exclusive position.

As a comparison, I would like to set alongside this example the architecture surrounding Dr. Wierwille's office. Green, rolling lawns, a patio terrace, a door directly from the patio into the office. How much more available and accessible can a person make himself? Someone decides to see Dr. Wierwille, approaches the door and is waved inside.

I set these examples side by side to show you how architecture defines space and can make us feel a certain way about ourselves and other people. If architecture has this potential inherent in it, can we not also think through the forms to make it bring out the qualities God's Word states about His people? Yes, of course.

Hitler, with spiritual help, understood and worked to capture the imaginations, the souls, the minds of the German people in the 1930s. Ideas control people. His message, his words of German supremacy, of militarism, national pride and conquest were reiterated through all the arts around him—visually, musically, verbally. Films, paintings, sculptures, architecture—all were calculated to fill the whole imagination, all five senses, with the reality and importance of his message. Early in the thirties he established Hitler schools, Hitler camps, Hitler youth, Hitler everything.

Here is a recent example of the transformation of an entire culture through the institutions and arts of that society. In thirteen years, roughly between 1930 and 1943, the culture of Germany was totally changed to manifest the message. From 1943 to 1945, the products (goods and services) of that same culture were all but totally destroyed: the architecture, art, movies, schools, theatres, etc. and also the people whose imaginations had been filled with the detailed fullness of Hitler's dream.

For me, this example from history shows once again: it is available. Culture can be transformed and it need not take hundreds of years or even two generations. It can begin now and be carried out quickly. This particular transformation was built on a man's words, on many obvious lies, on inconsistencies, on confusion. But by working in details on people's minds, through the arts especially, Hitler bought these people's souls. They believed. They backed him and became committed, many of them even to their deaths. Yes, he had spiritual help from the adversary to have been able to move so quickly. But where did the adversary get his information? Why, he used principles that work, principles from the Word of God!

These same principles are available to us. But we are not forced to use them toward evil ends. No, we have the pleasure of discovery, of utilization, of working, of implementing them by our own free will, to build that high degree of excellence with God our co-worker. We are not forced, or possessed, or terrorized into bringing about change. But in working it all through, from thought to finished product, we have the joy, the learning, the growth, the sweetness of accomplishment, the inspiration of seeing God work to teach us. BUT WE MUST THINK!

Our content, the unspeakable riches of Christ in us, is utterly unsearchable, but it is communicable. And God has limited Himself to our carrying forth of His Word in this administration. We are His hands, His feet, His mouth.

So we as artists have the same ministry of reconciliation, the same Word of reconciliation as every other born-again believer. God has fearfully and wonderfully made us. He has provided us with five wonderful senses and with the exhortation to be imitators of Him.

He has been and still is the Doer, the Maker, the Creator. We desire to put things together, great works that will allow God to work in us and teach us as we apply knowledge, and to have the opportunity to inspire love, inspire believing, inspire hope, to share the Word in some way that especially blesses us.

In the essay, "On Writing," I have cited the verse from Habakkuk 2:2 which I believe summarizes the what, how and why, not only of writing, but also of all the arts which were and still are designed to move God's Word.

Habakkuk 2:2:
And the Lord answered me, and said, Write the vision, and make *it* plain upon tables, that he may run that readeth it.

As artists in any phase of the arts, *what* we write, sing, dance, dramatize, play, paint, draw, photograph, build, design, etc.—is VISION, some aspect of God's vision for us in this administration. Vision is what is available from God's point of view. All the arts are to build vision.

How we write, sing, dance, dramatize, play, paint, draw, photograph, build, design, etc., is to be plain, simple, easily grasped, readily understood. We, as artists, do and make so that the vision can be received.

Why do we write, sing, dance, dramatize, play, paint, draw, photograph, build, design, etc.? So the receiver, our audience, will run the race for God, stay in fellowship with renewed commitment, dedication, inspiration and insight.

We as artists have the privilege through our various media to move the Word in God's people so that they move God's Word.

What is available for us? Read the Word, get vision, speak in tongues, study and think. Think. Reckon. Think through the forms.

How do we receive? I have not even touched on this at all—have not mentioned the action, the work of it, the specific study, the detail of the skills, the hours of practice, the concentration, the sweat in the actual accomplishment. It is all there, but if you find pleasure in doing it, the task is no burden. As we produce, we are receiving, learning, growing, understanding God and how He works with us specifically, deliberately, patiently.

As we do, and do faithfully, we learn the ways of God. And what do we do with it when we have it? A form can be utilized to its best, or misused. If I leave you with one plea on my lips, having shared these thoughts with you, it is this: Please when you take the pen in hand, do not use it as a toothpick. Use it to write.

Essay Five

To Begin

Not a few times I have thanked God that I have only two feet—not three, or four, or five or more. Walking is very simple with only two feet. We put one forward, then the other. There are no other feet to choose from.

Even so simple is our walk with God. In our walk with Him, we have only two feet. Of our three parts—body, soul and spirit—there are two parts within our power to operate every second of our lives no matter where, with whom or how we are physically. If we are alive (and not alseep or comatose), these two feet of our walk with God are in our absolute power, no matter what our physical situation is.

We have absolute power to operate the spirit of God within us by speaking in tongues (the other eight operations require specific conditions, or other people), and we have absolute power to operate our minds. So the two feet of our walk with God are speaking in tongues and thinking His thoughts. And to walk, we can choose at any second to begin one or the other, and then to begin again, and again and again. A long string of beginnings results in continuity, faithfulness. And so we walk, one foot and then the other. Begin now to

231

speak in tongues. It is within your power. Begin now to think His thoughts. You are walking. Walking with Him.

Operating the spirit of God within us is the power base of our walk, but our thoughts direct the distribution of that power. Without our thoughts (renewed mind), our power will not come into evidence in detail. So the two feet of our walk with Him. We are born to live and born again to serve. We serve God by walking with Him.

These essays have concentrated on that point through which we must all pass, the place at which we actually make His thoughts our own. The point at which we are no longer merely mouthing them, but where His ideas are our own ideas, His thoughts, our own thoughts; where His dreams, aspirations and desires are our very own. For, as I stated in the first essay of Part Two, if our thoughts are His thoughts, we will be able to do nothing but speak and act and do His will.

In retrospect I would call these essays the three R's of getting God's Word in mind: Reading, Writing and Reckoning. My heart's prayer is that these thoughts and exhortations will inspire you to think His thoughts in new, different, more meaningful dimensions, that you will be inspired to apply God's Word in your daily life in ways you had not recognized before. It is in its application that God's Word becomes our very own, engrafted in our hearts.

Even as I sat writing in solitude, leaning my elbows on this gnarled, oak table in pale winter sunlight, I knew that one day you would be with me. I knew we would have fellowship together here around the warm glow of the fire of God's living Word. Thank you for sharing with me this adventure of walking with Him, one foot and then the other. I have rejoiced in your company. And now, let us both begin again.

Edgar Degas (1834–1917), *The Rehearsal*. Copyright The Frick Collection, New York